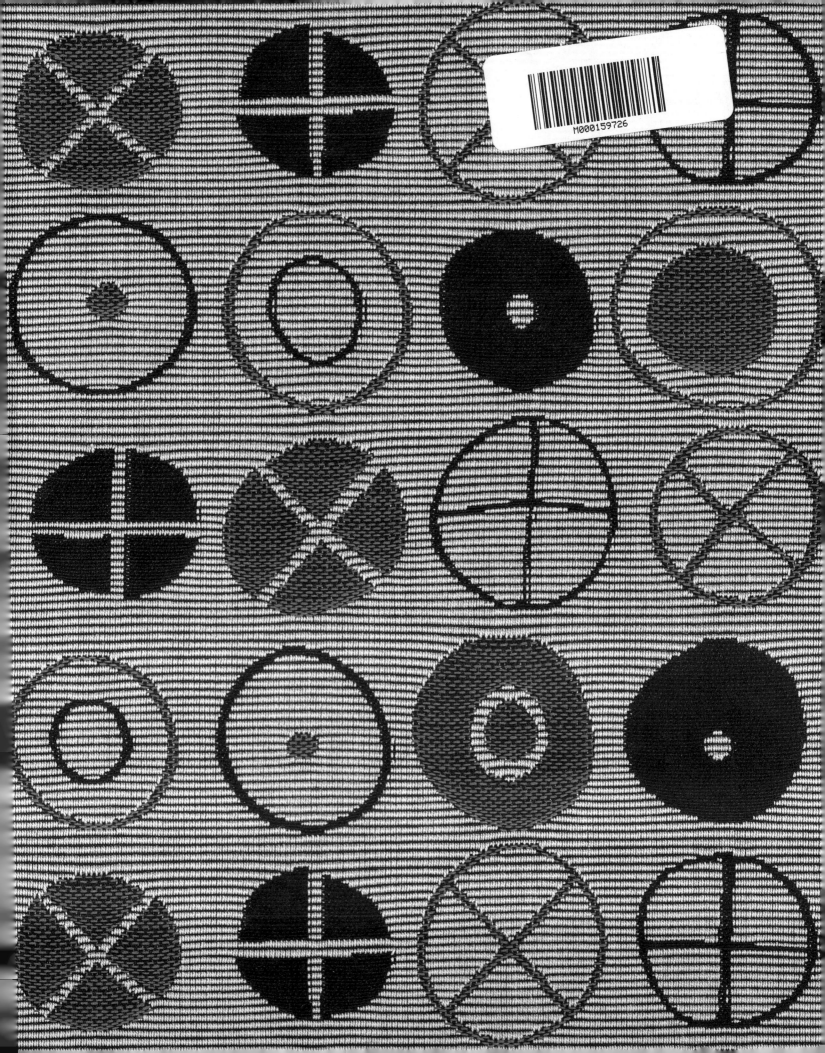

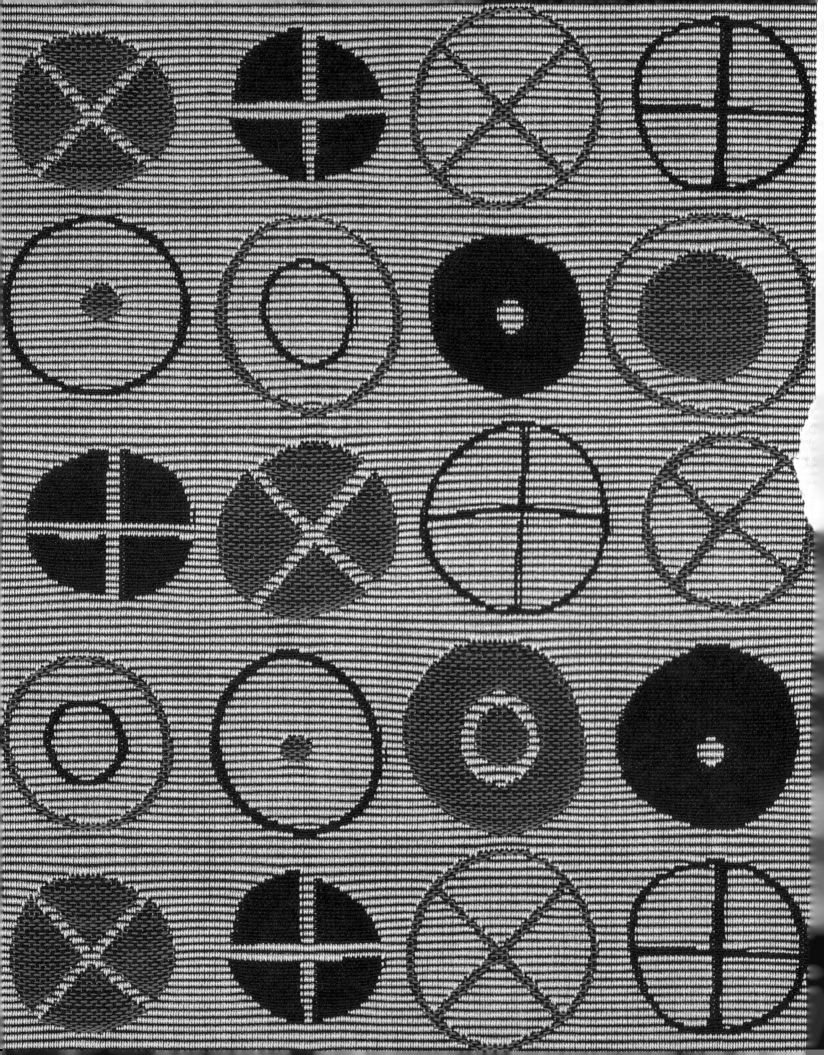

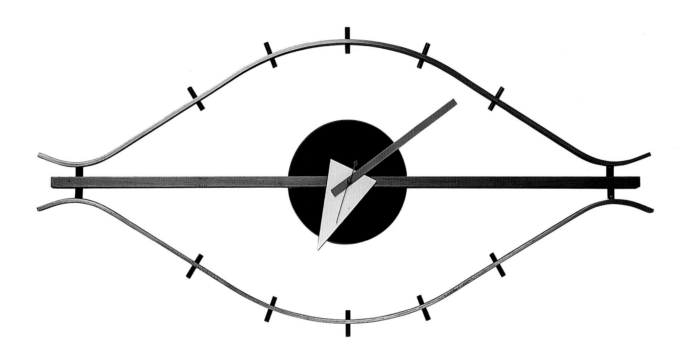

DEBORAH K. DIETSCH

midcentury modern

AN ARCHETYPE PRESS BOOK

classic modern

at home

SIMON & SCHUSTER

NEW YORK · LONDON · TORONTO · SYDNEY · SINGAPORE

contents

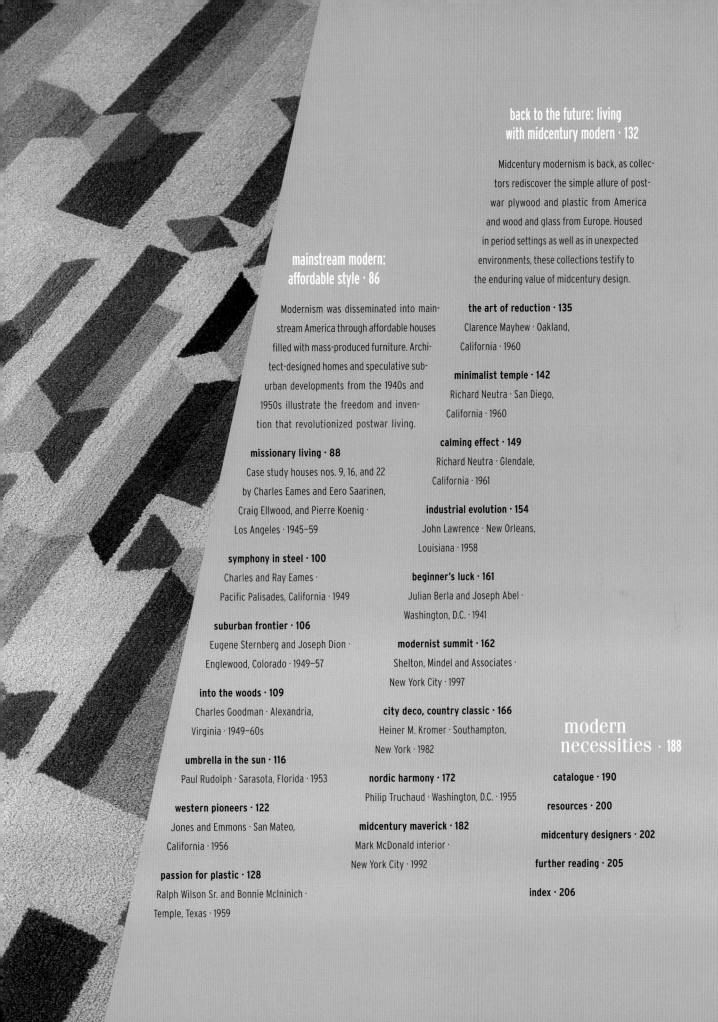

the essence of modern

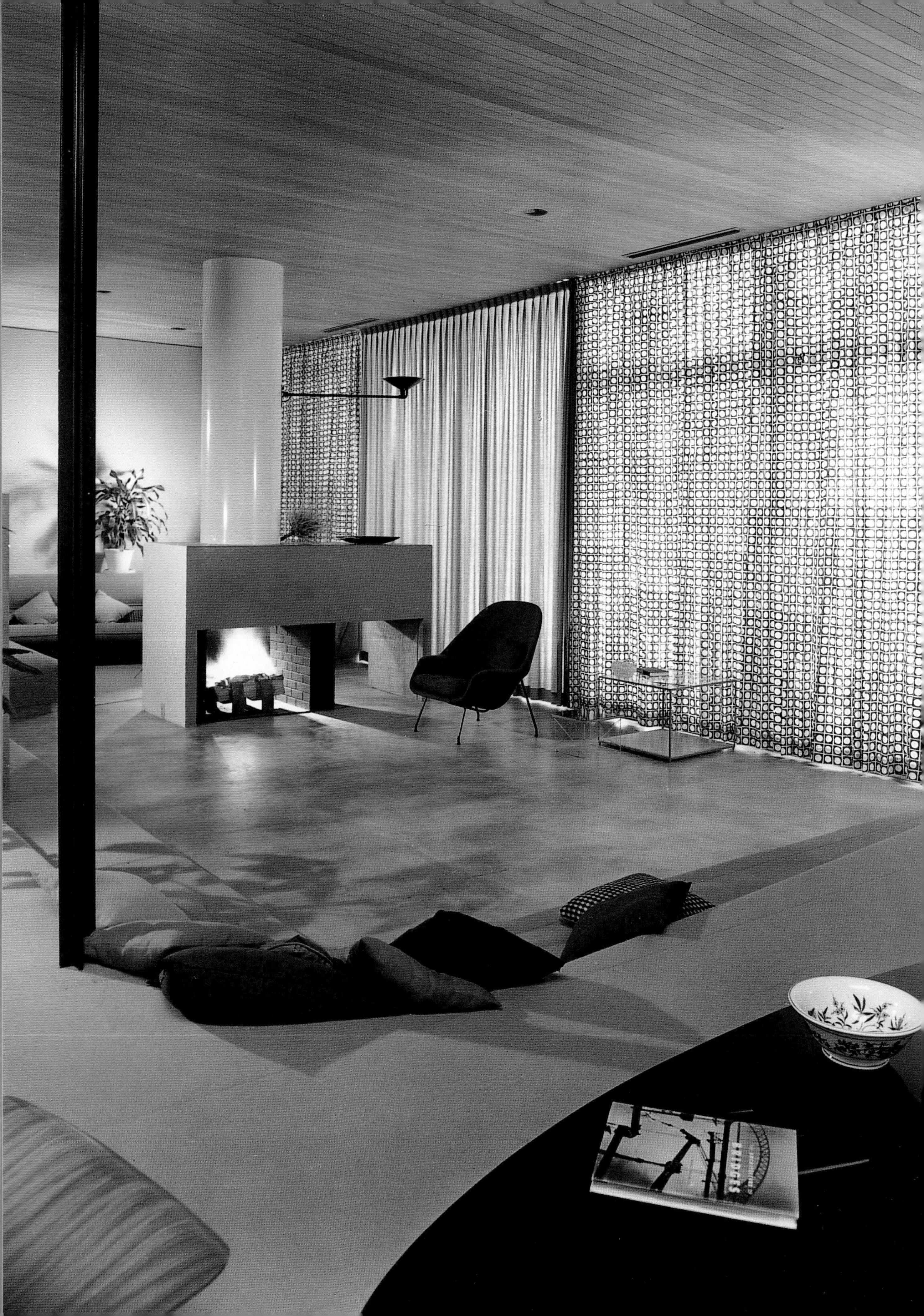

model houses, modern dreams

The decades after World War II launched a new age of confidence and optimism in many parts of the world. Unprecedented prosperity led to a consumer boom in both America and Europe that allowed ordinary people from California to Copenhagen to live better than ever before. The buildings and interiors designed in the late 1940s and the 1950s reflected a renewed, forward-looking spirit in airy, open spaces and clean-lined furnishings. Rooted in the modern movement of the early twentieth century, the period's most innovative designs were developed for the most basic and personal of buildings—the home.

Houses became the world's design laboratory for a simple reason: there was a dire need for new living units as millions of soldiers returned from the war to start careers and families. In the United States, for example, the Great Depression and the war had slowed housing starts; in 1944 a mere 114,000 new single-family houses were built. The shortage was so acute in some cities that Quonset huts, cars, chicken coops, and street trolleys were converted into temporary shelter.

The construction industry quickly responded by building houses using fast-track methods developed during the war. Leading this effort was the builder William Levitt, who applied assembly-line methods to manufacture a subdivision in Hempstead, Long Island. Levittown, as the community came to be known, was an instant smash. Thousands of two-bedroom, one-bathroom houses sold for $7,990, and for the first buyers, the developer threw in a television and a washing machine. As new roads and highways opened up vast tracts of land outside American cities, other builders soon copied Levitt's formula. Buying a house became as easy as buying a car.

Although the spare spaces of modern houses proved too severe for many buyers in the 1940s and 1950s, today's collectors have rediscovered them. This California house by Richard Neutra is now home to classic furnishings such as Russell Woodard's outdoor dining set and George Nelson's 1955 Coconut chair.

The huge demand for new housing led architects and suburban developers to propose a change in style to go along with the change in attitude. Modern warfare helped promote modern design by fostering acceptance of experimental materials and technologies. Buoyed by the victory of war and a booming economy, many consumers were attracted to the idea of starting afresh in spaces as sleek as a fighter plane. Modern men and women, after all, deserved something more daring than a cozy cottage and a picket fence. Even Levitt considered hiring the California modernist Richard Neutra to design some houses but concluded that the Viennese émigré's flat-roofed, stripped-down architecture would not sell.

Proponents of the modern house took advantage of consumer confidence to boost their cause. They played up its associations with openness and freedom, comparing glassy walls and rooms without barriers to the ideals for which the war was fought. "A continuing struggle for growing liberty" is how the architectural historian Talbot Hamlin characterized modern architecture in a 1945 issue of *House and Garden*.

Similar support of the avant-garde had been championed decades earlier. In 1932 New York's Museum of Modern Art staged an exhibition, *The International Style,* to publicize the progressive housing designed by architects in Europe. Just a few years later, three of those founding fathers of modernism—Walter Gropius, Marcel Breuer, and Ludwig Mies van der Rohe—departed Nazi Germany for academic jobs in the United States and soon opened their own offices. They joined other European architects who had come to America in the 1920s and 1930s—Neutra and R. M. Schindler from Austria, Eliel Saarinen and his son Eero from Finland, Albert Frey from Switzerland—to spread the gospel of high modernism.

The arrival of these important figures from the European modern movement helped create a climate of change. Influenced by their example, a younger generation of American designers began pushing modernism in a new direction. From Charles Eames in California to Paul Rudolph in Florida, architects developed a streamlined vocabulary that was less exacting than the severe white boxes of the Bauhaus. Their lightweight, modular houses, often built from standardized components and synthetic materials developed during the war, symbolized the era's buoyant mood. Flexible, flowing interiors and a strong indoor-outdoor relationship added to the dynamism of their structures.

Paul Rudolph's 1953 Umbrella House in Sarasota, Florida (opposite), epitomizes the uncluttered midcentury look. The modular sofa by George Nelson and steel-wire chairs by Harry Bertoia reflect an experimental attitude toward furniture—in contrast to Nelson's more traditional 1948 armchairs and sofa in a 1951 Richard Neutra house in Pacific Palisades, California (above). Neutra and other European émigrés nonetheless inspired the younger generation.

Instrumental in promoting this new approach were publications such as how-to books and decorating guides. Particularly influential on the West Coast was *Arts + Architecture,* a Los Angeles–based magazine edited by John Entenza. In 1945 Entenza sponsored a program he called Case Study Houses to encourage new ways of thinking about postwar living. Manufacturers donated prefabricated components for the prototypes' construction in hopes that such systems would be embraced as economical alternatives to wood and brick. The public was invited to view the houses before they were occupied.

Elegantly minimal, the Case Study Houses represented some of the most sophisticated architecture of the postwar era. Many of the projects were published in European magazines and copied abroad. But their modernism never took hold among builders and buyers. Most of the prototypes were built in steel, a material demanding more skilled labor than wood required, and thus were too expensive for the average homeowner. The era's economy favored the cookie-cutter approach of suburban builders, which did not allow much room for individualistic expression. By 1955 Levitt-style subdivisions accounted for seventy-five percent of new housing starts in the United States.

Although industrial-looking on the outside (left), the most famous of all the Case Study Houses—no. 8, completed in 1949 by Ray and Charles Eames— was made comfortable inside with the couple's own furniture designs, including their 1956 leather lounge chair and ottoman (above). Paperweights, dolls, toys, candlesticks, textiles, and other colorful souvenirs from their world travels filled their house (opposite).

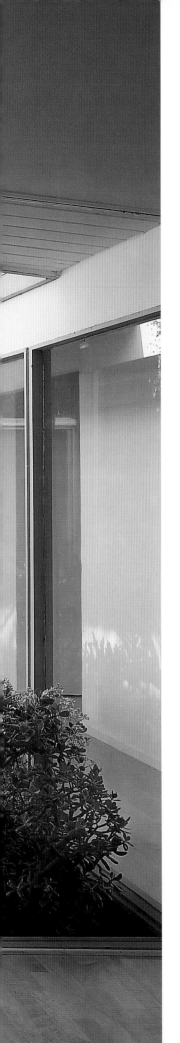

Despite the public's preference for Cape Cods and colonials, several leading home builders successfully adapted modern architecture to the mass market. Joseph Eichler and Edward Hawkins, both admirers of Frank Lloyd Wright, introduced fluid, indoor-outdoor spaces and structural expression to subdivisions outside San Francisco and Denver. Robert Davenport similarly applied a modernist vocabulary to tract housing in a suburb of Washington, D.C. On the west coast of Florida, Philip Hiss built second homes with flat roofs, overhangs, and canopies for vacationing midwesterners.

Where modern design made the most impact was inside the home. In the 1950s liberal, middle-class Americans relaxed on organic plywood and fiberglass chairs, dug their toes into Scandinavian rya rugs, dined on sculptural ceramic dishes, and swiftly cleaned their plastic-laminate-topped tables. Promoted by the Museum of Modern Art and sold by leading department stores, much of this "good design" was created by young architects and designers who had helped the war effort. They eagerly applied materials and methods used in military applications to create light and comfortable furniture that mirrored the shape of the human body, such as the molded-plywood and fiberglass chairs of Charles and Ray Eames and Eero Saarinen.

Suburban developments and mass-produced furniture introduced the average consumer to affordable modern design. The most prolific developer was the California builder Joseph Eichler, whose trademark was a landscaped atrium (left). Among the most popular postwar furnishings were the Eameses' molded-plywood chairs (below), developed from their wartime experiments with leg splints. Produced by Herman Miller from 1946 to 1958, these chairs were put back into production in 1994. Isamu Noguchi designed the 1954 table.

The appeal of Scandinavian furnishings grew from its combination of natural materials and sleek forms, as reflected in the Danish designer Poul Kjaerholm's wicker-and-steel lounge chair (above) and Arne Jacobsen's Swan and Egg chairs (right) at Copenhagen's SAS Royal Hotel. Such elegant pieces refined the body-conscious designs of the Eameses and George Nelson, which Herman Miller showcased in 1960 (below).

While American at heart, the midcentury era also spawned innovations abroad as countries throughout Europe rebuilt their industries after the war. Scandinavia, in particular, produced modern furniture, textiles, glassware, and ceramics. Based on handicraft traditions, exports such as Danish teak furniture appealed to a wide spectrum of Americans as a bridge over the gulf between contemporary and conventional styles.

Leading European architects, like their American counterparts, became involved in the design of furnishings, treating the engineering of chairs, tables, and cabinets as seriously as buildings. In 1952, for example, the French architect Jean Prouvé, who had devised innovative prefabricated building systems after the war, collaborated with the designer Charlotte Perriand and the artist Sonia Delaunay to devise colorful shelving for student housing in Paris. Some custom-designed pieces were subsequently put into production. The Danish architect Arne Jacobsen created his curvaceous Egg and Swan chairs in 1958 for the SAS Royal Hotel in Copenhagen, but they were soon mass produced by Fritz Hansen.

American and European companies also began commissioning architects to create furnishings for instant mass production. In 1941 Hans Knoll tapped Jens Risom to create a line of chairs with upholstery woven from parachute webbing. Five years later, Herman Miller appointed George Nelson as its first design director, beginning a long tradition of product innovations. In the early 1950s the Italian architect Gio Ponti created chairs to be made by Cassina as well as glassware for Venini, bathroom fixtures for Ideal-Standard, and a host of decorative objects for other companies. Soon furniture design emerged as a profession in its own right. Leading specialists included the English designer Robin Day, who won MoMA's 1948 competition for low-cost furniture, and his wife, the textile designer Lucienne Day. Through their work for Hille and Heal's, they came to be regarded as Britain's version of Charles and Ray Eames.

In addition to furnishings, midcentury design's greatest influence was on the planning of the house. By the mid-1950s ideas that modern architects had proposed in the late 1940s had trickled down to standard-issue suburban homes. Kitchens were the biggest recipients of high-style experiments, becoming larger and more open with push-button appliances built into the walls. Living rooms turned more informal and often incorporated the dining area into one unobstructed space. Spawned by the proliferation of television sets, the family room emerged from the basement as a second living room on the house's main level.

The average homeowner, however, never wholeheartedly embraced modern design. Sensing the public's distaste, magazines began denouncing what *House Beautiful* Editor Elizabeth Gordon called the "stripped-down emptiness" of the International Style. "No wonder you feel uneasy and repelled," wrote Gordon in "The Threat to the Next America" in the April 1953 issue. "They [architects and designers] are trying to convince you that you can appreciate beauty only if you suffer." Voicing concern over the "unlivability" of "modernistic" homes, she pointed to the "self-chosen elite who are trying to tell us what we should like and how we should live." Gordon went on to characterize architects such as Mies van der Rohe and Le Corbusier as dictators seeking regimentation and control.

Modernism may not have been completely accepted at home, but it was considered an asset for businesses seeking power and prestige. By the 1950s the sleek glass-and-metal facade had become the preferred style of North American corporations. Early examples include the Saarinens' General Motors Technical Center (1956), Lever House (1952) by Skidmore, Owings and Merrill, and Mies van der Rohe's Seagram Building (1958). Inside these headquarters, desks were eventually replaced by office systems, derived from the modular shelving units designed for the home. What began as a domestic revolution soon spread to businesses, schools, government buildings, even churches. In war-torn Europe, entire towns and cities were rebuilt in the new modern mode.

Today this once-revolutionary style is considered historic. Mass-produced vintage furniture fetches record-setting prices at auction, and manufacturers have reissued classic midcentury designs. Houses filled with plywood and plastic laminates and entire subdivisions are being preserved as landmarks. This renewed interest is rooted in the appeal of an era marked by unparalleled energy and boundless possibility.

Kitchens with built-in appliances and cabinets, first introduced by progressive suburban developers such as Joseph Eichler in California (opposite), soon became standard features. Produced just in time for the era's open dining areas, Heywood-Wakefield's transitional but streamlined wooden pieces (above) became America's fastest-selling modern furniture in the 1940s.

the midcentury look

The midcentury look was more an attitude than an aesthetic. As modernists, postwar architects and designers derived the style of their buildings and furnishings from materials and construction techniques rather than from applied decoration. But they adopted a more relaxed attitude toward the form-follows-function credo of earlier decades. Idiosyncrasies of clients, sites, and building materials were no longer seen as obstacles— they were catalysts for more creative and individualistic design.

The monotony of flat roofs, stucco walls, and horizontal windows of the 1920s and 1930s was discarded in favor of more diverse expressions. Roofs were pitched as well as flat. Exterior walls were paneled in wood, brick, steel, or combinations of materials. Windows were kept small or expanded into sliding panels of glass. Interiors were arranged as a series of continuous spaces rather than divided by hallways into separate rooms. They were often connected to terraces and gardens by glass perimeter walls that formed a transparent barrier between indoors and out. As a result, the rear yard was often treated as a series of outdoor rooms with patios and canopies extended from interior living spaces.

A house was viewed as a flexible system of elements tailored to the climate and topography of a specific site. These practical concerns led to regional variations of the modern idiom. The Case Study Houses built in the arid hills of Los Angeles, for example, were framed in steel filled with uninterrupted walls of glass to capture the view, while the residences designed by the Sarasota School on Florida's west coast were built of wood and outfitted with jalousie windows to capture cool breezes.

Furnishings assumed a new role as space dividers and modular systems that could be taken apart, added onto, and moved from room to room. Wall paneling and flooring in different materials similarly helped define different functions within a single space. Bright colors, patterns, and textures were applied to finishes and furniture to soften spare, uncluttered spaces.

The rise in disposable income during the postwar period led to a proliferation of new objects for the home, from lightweight, curvilinear furniture to imported glass and ceramics. Personal expression was encouraged and made possible by inexpensive, mass-produced consumer items. Even in traditional homes, modern elements such as plastic-laminate countertops and storage dividers between rooms became practical alternatives to the old-fashioned designs of the past.

Open shelves between the kitchen and the dining area in a 1955 home in Washington, D.C., achieve the flowing spaces typical of postwar modern interiors. Eero Saarinen's fiberglass Tulip table and chairs from 1956 are among the most well known of the lightweight, organic furnishings that filled midcentury houses.

flowing spaces, casual living

Light and airy, the midcentury modern house catered to a casual way of life. Interior spaces flowed into one another, rather than being divided into separate boxes connected by hallways—a legacy of Frank Lloyd Wright and early modernists. Even the smallest home appeared spacious.

These open plans were made possible by structural-engineering advances that came during the first decades of the twentieth century. Buildings no longer required heavy walls for support, only a skeletal frame that allowed partitions to be independent of structural elements. Activities could be separated by impermanent barriers or none at all.

Living and dining rooms often shared the same space, differentiated mainly by the furniture. The living area was often linked to the kitchen by a pass-through opening or a countertop with stools for informal dining. In some cases, only a change in finishes identified different functions: vinyl tile and plastic laminate in the kitchen, wood flooring and paneling in the living and dining areas. Furnishings played a major role as a screening device: movable storage units, bookshelves, and cabinets divided the living space from the dining area or the study. Fireplaces were also strategically placed to sequester living areas from adjacent activities.

Changes in floor levels further subdivided different areas. In the 1957 Miller House in Columbus, Indiana (see pages 68–73), for example, Eero Saarinen created a separate lounge area within the open living room by sinking upholstered seating into a fifteen-square-foot pit. Privacy was maintained in the open-plan house by locating bedrooms and bathrooms in their own wings. But in two-story houses, even such intimate spaces were connected to living areas by mezzanines and balconies. In their 1949 house in Pacific Palisades, California (see pages 100–105), Ray and Charles Eames positioned the bedroom on a mezzanine overlooking the double-height living area.

Wherever possible, midcentury houses embraced nature and made the outdoors into another room. Inside merged into outside, instantly annexing more space. The Bay Area developer Joseph Eichler took advantage of California's temperate climate to build his houses (see pages 122–27) around a landscaped atrium. Multipurpose and flexible, the open-plan house could be changed as families—and pocketbooks—grew.

Richard Neutra blurred the distinction between outdoors and indoors in his 1946 Palm Springs, California, house for the Kaufmann family. He opened the dining room (above) to a breezeway screened by louvers and transformed the rooftop into a shaded outdoor living room with a fireplace (right).

transparent barriers

WINDOW WALLS · SLIDING-GLASS DOORS · LIGHT-FILLED ROOMS

Walls of glass lightened the modern house. Architects first widened windows into continuous panes in the 1920s and 1930s. Like a thin skin wrapping the building, these glass ribbons were often set flush with the facade. By the 1940s they had grown into large sheets of plate glass, made possible by new technologies. Picture windows dominated living rooms, and floor-to-ceiling glass with sliding doors opened onto patios. Allowing daylight to penetrate the innermost reaches, these transparent barriers forged a seamless connection between indoors and outdoors.

Few architects were as skilled in establishing this inside-outside relationship as Richard Neutra. For his Kaufmann House in Palm Springs, California, Neutra eliminated supports and mitered the corners of his glass walls. Without frames or mullions to block the view, the windows virtually disappeared to unite house and landscape as a continuous space. Such transparency had been favored by European architects since the 1920s. The Danish architect Arne Jacobsen, for example, won a design competition in 1929 for a glass-enclosed circular house. Jacobsen's winning scheme turned into reality when he reconfigured his Round House in 1957 for the owner of a fish-smoking factory in Odden, Denmark.

Such glassy surfaces required skillful orientation to the sun's path. Louvers, canopies, and other screening devices were often installed to control solar rays and maintain privacy. Neutra used vertical fins of light-reflecting aluminum to shield the Kaufmann House's window walls. Other architects filtered daylight with corrugated, patterned, and float glass. Craig Ellwood designed his Case Study House no. 16 (1952) in Los Angeles (see pages 92–95) with freestanding panels of translucent glass that screen the south-facing bedrooms from the sun and the street.

With huge windows framing the view, the garden became as important as the house. Landscapes were an extension of the open plan, translating modern architecture's planar elements into walls, pools, planters, and vegetation. Defined by hedges and trees, Dan Kiley's garden for the Miller House in Columbus, Indiana, extended the pinwheel plan of Eero Saarinen's architecture into the landscape. Through glass walls, Saarinen's open plan flowed uninterruptedly from interior to terrace, garden, and meadow. Architecture locked nature in a strong embrace.

Floor-to-ceiling windows and skylights allow sunlight to penetrate the pie-shaped rooms of the Danish architect Arne Jacobsen's Round House in Odden, Denmark, built finally for a client in 1957. These windows are typical of the generous walls of glass that surrounded midcentury modern building perimeters.

malleable materials,
mass produced

MOLDED PLYWOOD · FIBERGLASS · PLASTIC LAMINATE

A vast array of synthetic substances—acrylics, polyester resins, styrofoam, vinyl—revolutionized homes in the postwar decades. These chemical-based materials were developed for military uses during World War II as substitutes for scarce steel and aluminum, but they inspired civilian designers to explore new artistic frontiers.

Working for the navy, Ray and Charles Eames created splints for wounded soldiers from molded plywood and later bent the laminated sheets into furniture. Russel Wright produced a line of dinnerware using a plastic lining in army helmets called melamine formaldehyde. Eero Saarinen shaped his famous Womb chair from fiberglass—a reinforcement for radar domes—and filled it with foam rubber. Using malleable materials, fluid, multidirectional curves could be sculpted with machined precision, and chairs and sofas could be built with seats and backs that fit the human body without the need for traditional upholstery.

Wartime technologies made these innovations possible, but it was mass production that made them affordable. Furniture manufacturers such as Herman Miller and Knoll adopted the auto industry's assembly-line approach to fabricating products in large numbers at low cost. Soon, ordinary people began buying the plywood and plastic chairs developed by Eames and Saarinen.

Synthetic materials transformed not just furniture, but nearly every surface inside the midcentury home. Wipe-clean plastic laminate and vinyl replaced ceramic tile in the kitchen and bathroom. Latex paint, plywood paneling, and fiberglass draperies provided durable substitutes for traditional finishes and fabrics in living and dining rooms. Plastic plumbing fixtures and styrofoam insulation ensured comfort at a reasonable price.

Lightweight and easy to maintain, the new synthetics met the public's growing demand for convenience and leisure. By the mid-1950s plastics trailed only steel, lumber, and glass to become the country's fourth largest industry. Acceptance of these forward-looking materials was quick, given their progressive association with the brave new world of science.

Plywood and plastic laminate took over homes at midcentury. In a 1956 Bay Area house built by the developer Joseph Eichler (above), plywood fronts an Eames cabinet and laminate tops an Eames Elliptical table. In his Texas home (opposite), Wilsonart founder Ralph Wilson even applied his company's laminates to the walls of the living room, now furnished with a pair of plywood lounge chairs and a molded-wood-and-leather lounge chair, both by the Eameses.

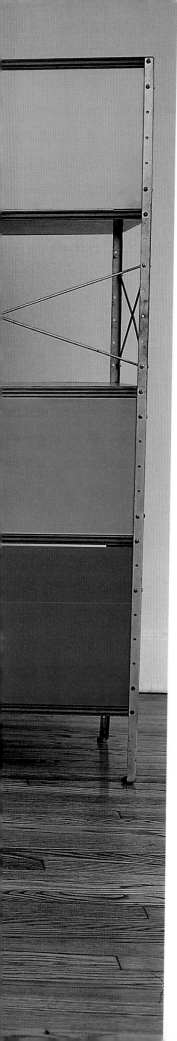

furniture of many uses

STACKING CHAIRS · KNOCK-DOWNS · MODULAR SHELVING · MOVABLE SCREENS

Lightweight and portable, furnishings of the 1940s and 1950s underscored the modern home's informality and openness. The heaviness of the Victorian era and even the 1920s and 1930s vanished. Steel tubing was flattened into narrow steel rods; wooden legs tapered into slender limbs. Plywood or plastic was molded into one seamless piece that seemed ready to float. Foam-rubber cushions replaced leaden upholstery. Screens stepped in lightly where walls once stood stolidly.

Rooms were no longer cluttered but carefully composed with free-standing pieces of furniture. Chairs, more movable than sofas, became increasingly popular, along with tables and cabinets that could be rearranged and adapted for more than one space and more than one function. "Eames chairs can be put into any position in an empty room; they look as though they had alighted there," the British architect Peter Smithson said about the curved shells on slender legs developed by the husband-and-wife team. "The chairs belong to the occupant, not the room." To save space, they could also be stacked and stored.

While American manufacturers promoted an industrial aesthetic through man-made materials, their Nordic counterparts stressed natural materials that appeared to be crafted by hand. Graceful chairs in teak, beech, and oak produced for specific buildings by Danish designers such as Arne Jacobsen, Hans Wegner, and Finn Juhl inspired affordable copies for export. Thanks to mass production, Scandinavian companies developed knock-down components that could be easily packed and shipped.

Flexibility extended to demountable storage walls that made the most of compact floor plans. Conceived as "systems," they consisted of shelving, drawers, and supports such as aluminum poles that could be rearranged and expanded. Although such modular units had been introduced in the 1920s by Le Corbusier and Marcel Breuer, they assumed a new practicality in the hands of midcentury American designers. In 1946 George Nelson created a combination cabinet and room divider for Herman Miller. The cabinets, perfect for storing books, tableware, or hi-fi equipment, could be placed on Nelson's slatted bench, on their own legs, or hung on a wall. This design was followed by Paul McCobb's popular Planner Group and the Eames Storage Unit, which had interchangeable drawers and panels set into a steel frame. Over the next two decades, modular home furnishings like these evolved into work stations for the office.

Manufacturers often offered a single design in various permutations to allow customization. Herman Miller produced the Eameses' 1950 fiberglass chair (left) with a choice of six bases and their 1950 Storage Unit with interchangeable panels. In addition to the couple's folding plywood screen from 1946, space-saving furnishings of the mid-twentieth century included Arne Jacobsen's 1955 Seven chairs (above) for Fritz Hansen.

textures nubby and plain

The rustic stone fireplace contrasts starkly with the smooth wood floors and plaster walls of a house in Southampton, New York (below). In the living area of a classic modern house in Hollin Hills outside Washington, D.C. (opposite), a brick fireplace plays the same role. Adding another layer of texture are furnishings by Paul McCobb, Eero Saarinen, and Heywood-Wakefield.

As architects adopted new materials in the 1940s and 1950s, a richer, less uptight modernism emerged from the austere functionalism of the 1920s and 1930s. Uniformly white walls gave way to varied surfaces modulated by color and texture. Even the strictest modernists began enriching their palettes.

"I have come to the conclusion," wrote Marcel Breuer in 1955, "that it is much more interesting, much more vigorous, much more 'human' if the colors are contrasted with a completely different element—with nature, or stone, or wood." Breuer practiced what he preached in a series of houses in the 1950s. Stone, brick, and wood siding clad the exteriors and came inside to cover walls, floors, and fireplaces, softening the rectilinear surfaces and tying them to the local vernacular. They also served to establish a seamless transition between outdoors and indoors.

This interplay between plain and textured surfaces dominated the mid-century modern home. Four or five finishes were often combined in the same room. Wood paneling and brick accompanied painted plaster walls. Fabrics, such as grass cloth, and printed wallpapers appeared as accents. Floor-to-ceiling glass windows, perhaps screened with draperies of nubby, open-weave fabrics, added another layer of texture.

In addition to natural materials, wood-grained plastic and colored laminates transformed walls and built-in surfaces as low-cost, low-maintenance alternatives. Ceilings were fitted with acoustical tiles to absorb noise. Floors in one room were covered in hardwood, stone, or terrazzo, and in another, tiles of cork, vinyl, or linoleum that fit the flexibility of the house's open plan.

Fieldstone walls, brick fireplaces, and other substantial materials anchored the era's lightweight, organic furnishings, which themselves expressed textural contrasts: plywood seats balanced on steel legs, fiberglass lamp shades perched on ceramic bases, and glass tabletops supported by wooden bases. Juxtapositions of materials called attention to each component of a design, heightening textural interest.

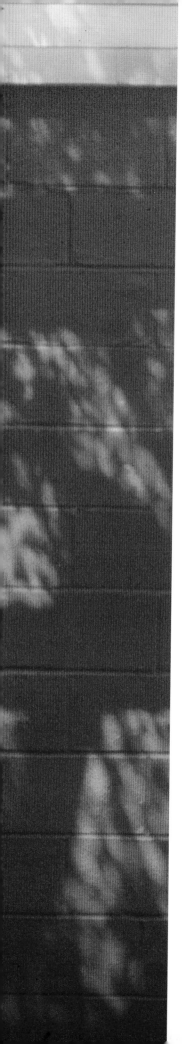

cheering colors
and bold patterns

Reflecting the verve and optimism of the 1950s, exuberant colors and patterns marked a radical departure from drab wartime interiors. Pigments developed for plastics, synthetic paints, and fibers initiated a brighter, clearer range of shades. Primary colors became popular as accents. Sharp hues—blue and green, pink and orange—were juxtaposed in startling contrasts. Such schemes were touted not only for their visual effects but also for their healthful consequences. "Cheering colors," claimed a 1954 home decorating guide, "lessen the apparent need for vitamins and tonics."

Color defined each surface in a room, much like an abstract painting in three dimensions. Architects began the practice in the early twentieth century by calling out the elements of their planar buildings in different primary shades. This color-coding assumed a new flexibility in postwar America. The Eameses applied a Mondrian-like palette to their steel-framed Case Study House and modular storage units, but with the suggestion that the colored panels could be switched around. Alexander Girard designed the sunken sofa in the Miller House in Columbus, Indiana, so that the fiery upholstery and pillows could be changed to cooler colors in the summer.

Patterned fabrics and interior finishes provided visual contrast against solid-colored walls and furnishings. Bold geometrics based on modern art and symbols of the atomic age replaced florals and representational motifs. International influences made their way into textiles. Girard designed a line of folkloric prints for Herman Miller based on his travels in Latin America. Jack Lenor Larsen developed hand-spun cottons and wools from Haiti and Mexico. Other companies imported Thai silks, Norwegian straws, and Swedish linens. Scandinavian rya rugs were prized for their shaggy textures and blurry, colored shapes.

Wallpapers and plastic finishes shared the same bright geometric and exotic patterns. By the 1950s Formica was marketing seventy-two choices in its line of laminates, including its celebrated boomerang-patterned Skylark. Such a wide—and affordable—range of colors and patterns allowed average homeowners to customize the decor of their homes with the latest modern look.

Calling for "the reddest red, the bluest blue, the yellowest yellow," Marcel Breuer painted the concrete-block walls of his 1953 Neumann House outside New York City in fiery red (left). Bold surfaces like these were good backgrounds for furnishings upholstered in abstract geometric prints, such as the atomic-age sofa (above) in a developer-built suburban house in Alexandria, Virginia.

curvaceous organic shapes

NATURAL FORMS · GENTLE CURVES · EVEN BOOMERANGS

To present an alternative to "vain ornamentation" and "out-of-date and rigid-ified furniture," the Museum of Modern Art in New York City staged a competition for well-designed and affordable furnishings in 1940. First place went to the architects Charles Eames and Eero Saarinen for seating and storage units that exemplified the contest's title: Organic Design in Home Furnishings. Their molded-wood chairs joined back, seat, and arms into continuous curves that conformed to the human body.

Advancing the bent-plywood designs introduced by Alvar Aalto and Marcel Breuer in the 1930s, the fluid shapes created by Eames and Saarinen flowed from new technologies. Chairs were first molded of wood veneers layered with plastic glue and then of fiberglass-reinforced plastic shells that could be left plain or padded. By 1956 Saarinen had replaced the four legs supporting the seat with a single stem to create his Tulip chair.

The same interest in nature-inspired forms extended to designers working in traditional materials. The American wood master George Nakashima produced both handmade and mass-produced furniture that underscored the innate structure of a tree. The Danish potter Axel Salto fashioned bulbous, richly glazed ceramics reminiscent of gourds, seedpods, and fruit. The French designer Serge Mouille created sculptural metal chandeliers with spiderlike arms reaching across the ceiling. The silversmith Henning Koppel, the first artist to join the Danish firm of Georg Jensen after World War II, hammered jewelry and flatware into exaggerated biomorphic shapes. Like Eames and Saarinen, these artisans based their organic designs on the physical properties of their materials. Their customized pieces, however, were more individualistic than the experimentalists' machine-made pieces—and harder to copy.

Whether handcrafted or manufactured, flowing forms became fashionable in both Europe and America. An entire spectrum of domestic products sprang up in the 1950s to satisfy the taste for organic design. Boomerang-shaped tables, rounded light fixtures, and swirling-patterned fabrics became popular household items. Symbols of a new informality, their gentle curves provided a humanizing counterpoint to the rigid angles of steel and glass that framed the modern home.

The Danish silversmith Henning Koppel's senuous pitcher (below), created in 1951 for Georg Jensen, reflects the biomorphic shapes beloved by Scandinavian designers in the 1950s. A kidney-shaped sofa and a drumlike fan in a Virginia house (opposite) show some of the curves applied to furnishings and appliances alike during the postwar period.

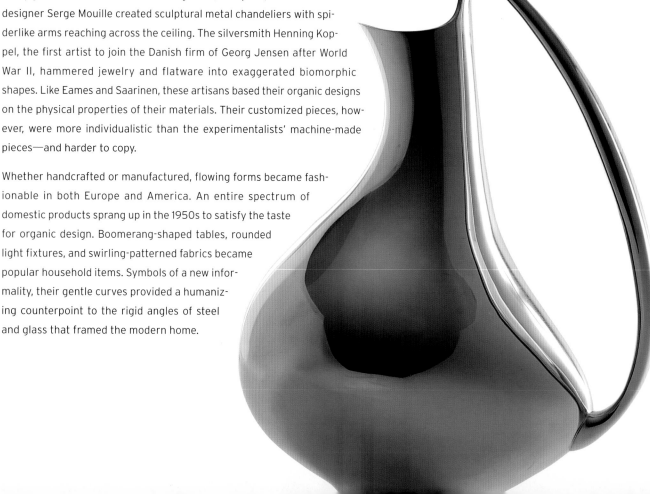

sculptural accessories

Freeform bowls, slender vases, and graceful decanters in the midcentury home reflected the same organic design that was being applied to furniture. They represented a new attitude toward glassware and ceramics. The Museum of Modern Art made the point in 1946, when it opened the show *Modern China by Eva Zeisel*. Presenting the expressive white dinnerware that it had commissioned from the Hungarian-born designer, the museum promoted the modern style in ceramics that had already taken hold in Europe.

Italy and Scandinavia led the way in developing sculptural glassware and pottery. The most progressive Italian glassmaker was Paolo Venini, who by 1945 had become the leading producer of colored glass. His simple shapes were enriched by a variety of decorative effects, such as patchwork and filigree patterns, and he often collaborated with Gio Ponti, Carlo Scarpa, and other leading architects.

From Scandinavia came even more innovative glassware after the war. Influenced by the humanizing modernism of Alvar Aalto—his undulating glass vases of 1936, in particular—artisans created sculptural vessels of unparalleled beauty. Designs ranged from Timo Sarpaneva's rounded vase, described as "the most significant object" of 1954 by *House Beautiful,* to Vicke Lindstrand's thick cylinders, encased with colorful abstract patterns.

Scandinavian ceramics were more subdued. Inspired by ancient Asian designs, potters such as Gunnar Nylund, Stig Lindberg, and Berndt Friberg preferred tapered shapes and matte glazes in muted earth tones. Despite industrialization, fine craftsmanship remained important. Large factories, such as Finland's leading manufacturer, Arabia, incorporated separate artists' workshops to encourage unique works for mass production.

Exported to the United States, Nordic art glass was considered a sophisticated touch in the American home. It led American manufacturers, such as Blenko, Viking, and Tiffin, to adopt curvaceous shapes and vibrant colors for their own glassware, often with the help of Swedish-trained artisans.

American ceramics, on the other hand, were less influenced by European finesse than by practicality. In 1946 Russel Wright produced his chip-resistant Iroquois Casual China with a one-year guarantee. Zeisel introduced her sensuous designs not only to MoMA but also to shoppers at Sears. Mass-produced dinnerware allowed the public to enjoy organic design at a reasonable cost.

Alvar Aalto's 1930s bent-plywood stool and undulating vase (opposite) paved the way for organic designs popular in the 1950s, such as Eero Saarinen's 1956 pedestal chairs seen on either side. The Finnish designer Timo Sarpaneva repeated the curvaceous theme in his 1954 Orchid vase (below left) and 1953 Devil's Churn vase (below right), both for littala.

midcentury modern at home

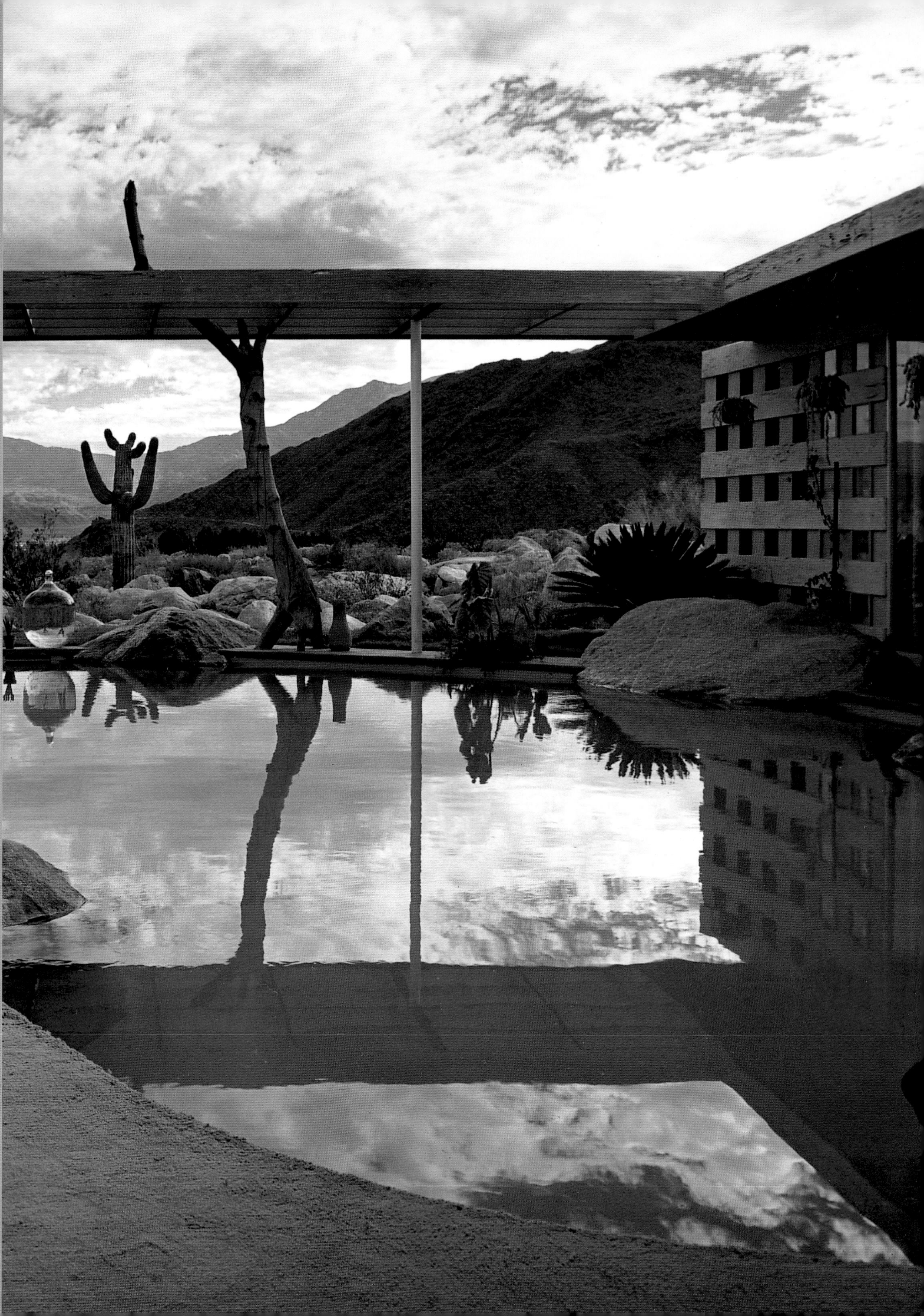

modern to the core: classic houses

European architects who emigrated to the United States around World War II seized the opportunity to pioneer new territory in an America ready for change. Leaders of the modern movement in Germany, France, Spain, and Scandinavia, they introduced their vocabularies of crisp facades, wide openings, and open-plan interiors to a country still getting used to the earth-hugging houses of Frank Lloyd Wright.

Several arrived to take up important academic posts, from which they influenced American architecture with their teachings. In 1938 the German architect Ludwig Mies van der Rohe fled Nazi oppression for Chicago to head what is now the Illinois Institute of Technology. Harvard had hired his Bauhaus colleagues Walter Gropius and Marcel Breuer the previous year, and in 1953 the university selected the Spanish architect José Luis Sert to succeed Gropius as dean of the Graduate School of Design.

Other Europeans fueled the progressive design of the postwar decades. The Swiss architect Albert Frey, who had worked for Le Corbusier, moved to California in 1939 and joined the Austrian émigré Richard Neutra in designing desert retreats. In the Midwest the Finnish-born Eliel Saarinen drew on Scandinavian craftsmanship to develop a cool rationalism, which his son Eero further expanded in the 1950s. The Danish designer Jens Risom applied the same craft tradition to furniture making in the 1940s and soon helped change the face of interior design.

The prosperity of the postwar years allowed these respected European masters to establish successful practices. Many went from planning experimental workers' housing to custom designing houses for doctors, department store owners, and corporate chieftains. Wealthy clients supported their Bauhaus rigor, encouraging avant-garde designs that drew critical acclaim.

Working in America, most of these Europeans were influenced by their surroundings. Site-sensitive gestures and regional touches in wood, brick, and stone replaced the white austerity of the International Style. The cold steel and taut leather of Bauhaus furnishings fit the interiors of their houses, but their architecture turned out to be equally welcoming to the experimental and lighter-weight household items that were rushed to market at midcentury. Widely published in the 1940s and 1950s, the Europeans' work gave prestige to the modern movement in America. These émigrés paved the way for a new generation of American architects who advanced their modernist ideas in a more humanistic direction.

From its glass walls and open rooms to its organic furniture—including laminated teak dining chairs and sofas designed for the SAS Royal Hotel in Copenhagen in the 1950s—Arne Jacobsen's 1957 Round House in Odden, Denmark, reflects many of the same ideas introduced by Europeans to America.

throwing a curve

ALBERT FREY · PALM SPRINGS, CALIFORNIA · 1946

No one was more responsible for creating the image of postwar corporate America than the French-born industrial designer Raymond Loewy. Among his iconic creations were the Coca-Cola bottle, the Lucky Strike cigarette package, Frigidaire refrigerators, the Greyhound bus, the Studebaker, and the Avanti. To get away from his prolific practice, Loewy decided to build "a small isolated house in the desert." In 1945 he hired the Swiss-born architect Albert Frey to design a retreat on a rocky site in the growing resort of Palm Springs, California.

Frey, who had worked for the French master Le Corbusier, had established a reputation for experimental architecture. After practicing in New York City and completing several small buildings in Palm Springs, he moved to the California vacation spot in 1939. His design shifted in response to the desert climate, from compact, cubic volumes to horizontal planes reaching out to the landscape. Working closely with Loewy, he organized the designer's house into an L shape around a courtyard and a swimming pool with half-submerged boulders. Around the pool, a redwood trellis connects the two ends of the one-story house to frame a panorama of the San Jacinto Mountains.

Surrounded by boulders, Raymond Loewy's house is arranged around a courtyard with a free-form pool. To harmonize it with the desert, Loewy—a designer himself—insisted on covering the courtyard-facing windows and trellis in pecky cypress, a pickled, worm-eaten wood. In 1948 he enclosed the original open-air solarium with glass panels for use as a dining room.

Inside, Loewy streamlined the living room ceiling with an aerodynamic curve. Frey, in turn, came up with the inventive idea of extending the pool—complete with one boulder—inside the living room just a few feet from the front door. The location surprised guests, including the actor William Powell, who accidentally fell in after arriving for a housewarming party.

In 1948 Loewy married and began expanding the house. He enclosed the open dining area with a curved glass wall, added a master suite off the bedroom wing, and built a freestanding studio on the southeastern edge of the property. Using the house as a winter vacation retreat, Loewy and his wife, Viola, filled it with simple furniture, shelves of ceramics and glass, and stones from the nearby Salton Sea. "Everything—including the furniture—is sand-colored, the exterior as well," wrote Loewy in his 1950 autobiography. "When the lights are off, the pool alone can be illuminated by a powerful submerged lamp, and the scene resembles a blue lagoon in a desert oasis."

After Loewy sold the property, Frey's design suffered alterations and neglect until 1995, when the current owners, Jim Gaudineer and Tony Padilla, began to reclaim the house. The partners, who own a Michigan-based metals company, turned to the Santa Monica architects Leo Marmol and Ron Radziner, who were in the midst of restoring Richard Neutra's Kaufmann House next door. Marmol and Radziner thought that Loewy's cypress-clad additions not only obstructed the view but also "blended in too well" with Frey's original structure. The architects reclad the studio and bedroom extension in buff-tinted cement plaster and added a glass-enclosed hallway topped by a sloping roof to connect the bedroom addition to the main house. This transparent connection now allows the mountains to be seen from the courtyard.

The current owners furnished the Loewy House with modern pieces such as a Mies van der Rohe lounge chair (left). From the courtyard, the swimming pool slides into the living area under glass doors (top). The canopied entrance (above) is set into a corrugated-metal wall extending into the landscape, a signature of Albert Frey. 49

Bertoia Diamond chairs and a Saarinen pedestal table frame the bedroom window (left). While the textured rug in the dining room was created in the late 1950s by a Michigan artist (above), the wrought-iron table belonged to Loewy. Wood mullions were replaced (opposite), but the original glass was preserved. Mies's Brno chairs and the Florence Knoll table are reproductions.

machine in the garden

RICHARD NEUTRA · PALM SPRINGS, CALIFORNIA · 1946

In creating a house in 1946 for Edgar and Liliane Kaufmann, Richard Neutra had a hard act to follow. Little more than a decade earlier, the Pittsburgh department store tycoon had commissioned Frank Lloyd Wright to design Fallingwater, one of the masterpieces of modern architecture. For their winter retreat in Palm Springs, California, however, the Kaufmanns sought an alternative to Wright's organic architecture: open living quarters that would rest lightly on the land. Edgar Kaufmann and Neutra, a Viennese émigré, collaborated intensely on the 3,200-square-foot, pinwheel plan of rooms separated by breezeways and patios. Crisply edged in steel, the glass-walled, cubic structure translates European modernism to the desert. To Neutra it was "a machine in the garden."

Although clearly man-made, the low-slung, planar house is sensitively oriented to its setting. Outstretched walls of Utah buff stone and plate glass protected by sun-screening louvers anchor the wings to the site while sheltering them from sunlight and dry winds. Carpetlike lawns and a rectangular swimming pool extend the building's geometries into the landscape. Neutra's skill in both floating and fusing his architecture with nature is perfectly captured in the photographer Julius Shulman's famous twilight image of the pool (see page 8). Taken in 1947, a year after the house was completed, it served as the inspiration for the house's meticulous restoration by its current owners, Brent and Beth Harris.

Atop the flat roof, a "gloriette" (a semi-enclosed terrace with a fireplace) provides space for entertaining (left). Walls protected by sun-screening louvers connect outstretched wings to nature while offering shelter. Between the living and dining areas (right), a breezeway incorporates a linear lily pond and strips of grass. All of the outdoor furniture is by Van Keppel–Green.

With its vintage Nelson bench, the entrance foyer (left) merges indoors and out with a continuous sandstone wall marked only by a thin barrier of glass. The master bedroom (right), overlooking the pool, is furnished with a Bruno Mathsson chaise and an Eames molded-plywood chair. Wool rugs were inspired by Joseph Blumfield originals from 1947.

By the time the Harrises bought the house in 1993, Neutra's design had suffered substantial alterations, including the addition of faux French Regency decorations by Barry Manilow, a previous owner. The Harrises enlisted the Santa Monica architects Leo Marmol and Ron Radziner to return the radically remodeled structure to its modernist glory. "It is one of the great modern houses," says Beth Harris, an architectural historian.

Guided by Neutra's original drawings and his correspondence as well as Shulman's historic photographs, they spent five years tracking down original finishes and fixtures. Determined pursuit led to a Utah quarry, where miners reopened a section so that the original rosy sandstone could be matched. A Missouri company reproduced the crimped sheet-metal fascias, and another firm in Los Angeles recreated missing custom light fixtures. To further protect Neutra's design, the Harrises purchased two adjacent lots and planted them to frame the spectacular views of the San Jacinto Mountains. Their ambitiously accurate restoration reinstates the tiniest details along with the house's sense of grandeur in the harsh desert landscape.

Flanked by metal-legged Eames dining chairs, the walnut dining table (left) was designed by Neutra for the house. The wool rug is reproduced from a Raymond Loewy design. To match the original, the cabinet was reveneered in birch. Kitchen countertops and floors (below) are covered in cork. Modern conveniences, from the television to exercise equipment, are housed in a new structure.

less is more

Floating in a field some fifty miles outside Chicago, the transparent Farnsworth House is one of the most radical houses ever built. Its rectangular glass box is sparingly outlined by eight steel columns and two horizontal bands of steel marking the floor and roof. The skeletal structure is the only American house to be completed by Ludwig Mies van der Rohe, the German architect who once headed the Bauhaus and emigrated to the United States in 1938.

Mies's client, Edith Farnsworth, worked in Chicago and sought a small weekend house on a piece of property she owned in Plano, Illinois. A single woman and a doctor, Farnsworth was as unconventional for her day as the house she commissioned. Mies took advantage of her solo status and the landscaped site to produce a severely austere design that pushed to extremes his dictum "less is more."

Radical in its minimalism, the house is more akin to a Greek temple than a domestic space. It is raised five feet off the ground to give the appearance of a refuge—and, more practically, to prevent flooding from the adjacent Fox River. An asymmetrically placed utility core, containing two bathrooms and a closet, divides the house's open main room from a galley kitchen. A dining space and a bedroom are placed at either end.

"I feel like a sentinel on guard day and night," Farnsworth complained to *House Beautiful* in 1953. "I can rarely stretch out and relax." The doctor, who eventually sued Mies over the escalated costs of the house, humanized the stark, transparent spaces with venetian blinds and antique furniture.

Newly restored, the Farnsworth House is furnished with reproductions of Mies's Tugenhat chairs and rosewood couch, as well as his original glass-topped table for the Barcelona Pavilion (left). After the house was flooded in 1996, the Chicago architect Dirk Lohan, Mies's grandson, replaced the primavera wood on the living room wall and the teak on the bedroom storage unit.

Furnished with Mies's 1927 tubular steel chairs, the dining area (above) faces a travertine terrace. The bedroom (right) is separated from the living area by a teak wardrobe. The stools are reproductions of designs for the Barcelona Pavilion. Completely sheathed in glass (opposite top), the house affords little privacy. It is entered from a staircase (opposite bottom) that rises to a patio.

Although derided in the popular press as "unlivable," the glass house was well received by professional journals and influenced leading architects of the day. Philip Johnson based his 1949 New Canaan house on Mies's design, and the Los Angeles–based Craig Ellwood adopted a similar steel-and-glass vocabulary for his Case Study Houses.

Despite its elevated position, the house was flooded in 1954, three years after its completion, and again in 1996. The second disaster broke the glass walls, washed away the furnishings, and covered the travertine floors with mud. "It was a wreck and needed drastic restoration," recounted Peter Palumbo, the London real estate developer who bought the house in 1972 and has since opened it to the public.

For the restoration, Palumbo tapped Mies' grandson, the Chicago architect Dirk Lohan. After cleaning the marble and replacing the glass, he replicated the damaged service core in its original primavera wood and rebuilt the teak wardrobe in the bedroom. Mies clearly triumphs in the house, which is now furnished with his furniture designs, including a black glass–topped table from his famous Barcelona Pavilion of 1929.

bauhaus, american style

MARCEL BREUER · CROTON-ON-HUDSON, NEW YORK · 1953

On a hill overlooking the Hudson River, a long, low building sits on a stone terrace with curved walls that follow the contours of the site. Concrete-block slabs painted in bright shades of red, blue, and white frame walls of wood and glass. The same palette of pure color also transforms the walls inside. As sunlight streams through the windows, the strong hues are reflected onto adjacent surfaces to bathe the rooms in a bright glow. River views appear from nearly every room.

Such masterful manipulation of space and light is the work of Marcel Breuer, the noted Hungarian-born architect who had taught at the Bauhaus and left Europe in 1937 to teach at Harvard University under his Bauhaus mentor, Walter Gropius. After collaborating on some residences, Breuer began to design single-family houses from his own office in New York City in 1946. While adhering to the Bauhaus aesthetic of ribbon windows and planar walls, he incorporated new regional touches, such as wood siding and rubble walls of local stone.

This American influence can be seen in this 1953 house built for George Neumann, a sculptor, and his wife, Vera, a fashion designer noted for her scarves. A central living-dining-kitchen area separates bedrooms at either end. Flagstone floors, cypress-paneled ceilings, and a free-standing white brick fireplace warm the spartan spaces.

Among current owner Barry Friedman's possessions is a 1957 Studebaker designed by Raymond Loewy (left). Dominated by a brick fireplace, the living room (right) is furnished with Bruno Mathsson's chaise and bent-plywood chair, an Eames plywood coffee table, a Nelson slatted bench, and a 1950s French rug. The slate floor extends to a terrace framed by a primary red wall.

The Neumanns owned the property until 1982, when they sold it to Patricia Pastor, a fashion designer who had worked for Vera, and Barry Friedman, a dealer in twentieth-century furniture and art. They could not have found more appreciative buyers: Friedman had long collected Breuer's furniture as well as premier examples of midcentury modern designs. "I've always been interested in the 1950s," he explains. "But when we bought the house, I got more interested."

After installing pieces that he already owned, Friedman went in search of more unusual furniture, as well as carpets, dishes, and silverware from the period. The house is now home to a curvaceous combination of American and European designs that happily coexist with Breuer's boxy built-in sofas and cabinets. In the living room, chairs of bent laminated wood by the Swedish designer Bruno Mathsson take their place alongside a plywood coffee table by Charles and Ray Eames. Quirky metal chairs by Dan Johnson, an American designer whose work was made in Italy, represent a cultural crossover.

In the children's bedrooms, the couple bifurcated the mix: their daughter's room is outfitted with furniture by the Eameses, George Nelson, and Isamu Noguchi, while their son's focuses on pieces by the French designers Jean Prouvé and Serge Mouille and the Scandinavian Greta Jalk. The art also reflects the period: drip paintings by the German abstractionist Helmut Zimmermann, a gouache by the mobile master Alexander Calder, and sculptures by the French artist Alexander Noll.

A guest house connected to the main structure by a canopied stairway was added by Breuer in 1972, together with an indoor swimming pool. The house is so well oriented to its site that it has no air conditioning, except for a bedroom unit. "In summer, the sun doesn't come in until 4 p.m., while in winter, it comes in all day," explains Friedman, who smiles at the thought of his low utility bills. "All houses should have been made like this."

In the dining room (opposite) is a wall-mounted cabinet designed by Breuer. Under a Poul Henningsen light fixture, the 1940s table is the work of Bruno Mathsson, and around it are Joe Atkinson's 1952 chairs for Thonet (detail above). A curvy 1950s French coat rack (below) expresses the same whimsy as the Eameses' Hang-It-All from 1953.

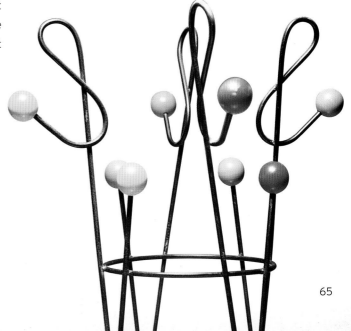

In the daughter's bedroom (above), Eero Saarinen's 1948 model chair for Knoll sits beside a sculptural wire-base table designed by Isamu Noguchi in 1954, also for Knoll, while the lamp and rug are French. The master bedroom (right) is furnished with George Nelson's 1956 Thin Edge beds and pedestal end table, both manufactured by Herman Miller.

modern monticello

The Finnish-born architect Eero Saarinen played an important role in shaping postwar design. At midcentury he produced such icons as Knoll's Womb chair (1948) and the cable-supported TWA Terminal at Kennedy Airport (1962). One of his most significant achievements, however, is his least known. In 1953 Saarinen designed a steel-and-glass house for J. Irwin Miller, chairman of the Cummins Engine Company, and his wife, Xenia. Located in Columbus, Indiana, fifty miles south of Indianapolis, the house was one of the first modern structures to be built in this architecture-rich town.

Over the five decades since it was completed in 1957, many other distinguished buildings by noted modern architects have been built in Columbus thanks to Miller's patronage. The industrialist first became involved with modern architecture when he persuaded his church to hire Eliel Saarinen, Eero's famous father, to design a modern sanctuary. Then in 1950 he tapped Eero to create the family's summer home in Ontario, Canada, and three years later for the Irwin Union Bank and Trust Company.

For his year-round residence, Miller sought a home that would "accommodate itself to the flat terrain" above the Flatrock River. Working with Kevin Roche, the project architect, Saarinen responded by raising the house on a low podium that forms a terrace around the house. Inside, he arranged separate quarters for the Millers and their five children as four "houses"—parents' and children's bedrooms, a guest wing, and a kitchen—all centered on an open living space. Sheltering the units is an enormous flat roof supported by steel columns and channels and fitted with skylights and artificial lighting. The roof projects over floor-to-ceiling glass walls opening onto raised terraces.

Saarinen turned over the interior design details to Alexander Girard, who enlivened the rigorous architecture with brightly colored rugs, pillows, and wall hangings. "He made the house a home," says Roche. "His sense of color was remarkable." Behind the cylindrical fireplace in the living room, Girard designed storage cabinets for the Millers' collection of antiques and art from all over the world. For seating, he sunk a fifteen-foot-square conversation pit into the floor. "The kids had overnight pajama parties in there," recalls Irwin Miller.

The view from the terrazzo terrace (opposite) outside the Millers' living area reveals Saarinen's structural rigor. Channels and skylights between the building and the roof overhang invite light inside. Walls are paneled in marble and slate. Enclosed by Dan Kiley with hedges, the pool area (below) features ivy beds around the podium and a leaping hare sculpture by Barry Flanagan.

While the house was under construction, the Millers hired the landscape architect Dan Kiley to plant the ten-acre property so that it would be private without walling off the neighbors. Building on his work for Hollin Hills, a suburb just outside Washington, D.C. (see pages 108–15), Kiley developed a geometric design as rigorous and spare as Saarinen's architecture. He extended the house's pinwheel plan into a series of green rooms screened by hedges and trees. In 1959 *House and Garden* compared the remarkable fusion of modern architecture and landscape to Thomas Jefferson's Monticello, "an enduring monument to American ingenuity, vision and craftsmanship."

Miller continued to influence Columbus's architecture by establishing the Cummins Engine Foundation, which pays the design fees for public buildings. Schools, firehouses, and other structures by innovative architects—many of them trained by Saarinen—have transformed the small prairie town into a mecca of modern architecture. With Miller's prodding, Columbus's world-renowned architectural roster is now etched with the names of such masters such as Cesar Pelli, Robert Venturi, Richard Meier, I. M. Pei, Harry Weese, and Edward Larrabee Barnes.

But the Miller house and garden won't be on any of the architectural tours. "We like our privacy," says the Hoosier industrialist, who still lives in the house with Xenia. Over the past five decades, the Millers have made few changes, except to upgrade the mechanical system and replace the skylights. "The house worked very well when we had five children," asserts Miller, now in his nineties. "And it still works well."

1956 Saarinen pedestal chairs and an eight-foot-diameter marble table are on stage in the Millers' dining room (above). At the table's center, a built-in bowl can be covered with glass, filled with flowers, or turned into a fountain. Water is pumped from a brass pipe in the base. The living room (right and opposite) is focused on a conversation pit that has marble coping and a teak stair.

Exuberantly patterned carpets (above and right) and drapes (opposite) were designed by Alexander Girard. Worn areas have been replaced with exact copies. The entranceway (right) is sky-lighted and furnished with a 1954 Eames Sofa Compact. One of the Millers' collections is displayed on the wall. Eames steel-wire chairs around the kitchen table (opposite) offer a view of Kiley's crab apple grove through a glass wall.

urban sanctuary

JOSÉ LUIS SERT · CAMBRIDGE, MASSACHUSETTS · 1958

For a small corner lot bordering the campus of Harvard University, José Luis Sert designed what he hoped would be a prototype for row housing on compact sites. The one-story house for himself and his wife, Moncha, was based on his schemes for cities in Latin America but tailored to Boston's northern climate with wood and brick. A follower of Le Corbusier, Sert enriched the more abstract European modernism by drawing on the arches, vaults, and courtyards of his native Spain to achieve sculptural, human-scaled forms.

Sert, who fled Franco's dictatorship in 1939, had built little before 1953, when he was named dean of Harvard's Graduate School of Design. The position gave him the opportunity both to teach and to design real buildings, many in Boston. To gain privacy for his own 1958 home, he returned to the age-old idea of the courtyard house and organized his design around three walled spaces: a large patio at the street, a twenty-four-foot-square atrium at center, and a garden courtyard at the rear. These roofless rooms extend the interiors outside, making the house appear larger.

Furnished with a 1950s table and chairs the new owners purchased in Denmark, the dining area (left) opens to the courtyard—the heart of the house—with its sculpture by Nina Holton. Sert's sculptural fireplace still frames the living area (right), now filled with 1950s Danish chairs as well as contemporary pieces. The fire wall acts as a subtle divider between the two main living areas.

A reproduction of a 1928 design by Le Corbusier and Charlotte Perriand, the leather-covered steel chaise longue (above and opposite) provides a comfortable perch for reading. The living room shelving follows Sert's concept. More shelves designed by Sert as well as an original accordion door mark a hallway (right). Nina Holton created the carved stone figure on the pedestal.

Inside, Sert conveyed a Mediterranean feeling with whitewashed walls and accents of red and blue on doors, window jambs, and the fireplace. Sliding-glass doors allow an uninterrupted view from front to back. In the living room, he angled the ceiling upward to clerestory windows and screened the adjacent dining area with a fireplace. To furnish the room, he designed low birch benches covered with brightly colored cushions. An avid art collector, the architect filled the house with paintings by fellow Spaniards Joan Miró (Sert had designed his studio in 1955) and Pablo Picasso.

After Sert's death in 1983, the house was rented until Harvard sold it in 1991 to Gerald Holton, a professor of physics and the history of science at the university, and his wife, Nina, a sculptor. Friends of the Serts, the Holtons had spent many evenings in the small courtyard home and were thrilled to become its new owners. "We always loved the house," says Nina Holton. "It's beautiful and simple. The rooms are filled with an extraordinary amount of light."

Renovations, carried out with advice from Sert's partner, Huson Jackson, ranged from transforming the garage into a studio to adding a living room storage cabinet based on Sert's original shelving in the entrance hall. Danish furnishings from the 1950s, purchased by the owners on a 1960 trip to Copenhagen, seem right at home. For the Holtons, their friend's humane design is welcome protection against the bustling campus and Harvard Square. "The courtyards have a monastic feeling," notes Nina Holton. "You enter the house and you leave all the noise behind you. It's a sanctuary."

Sert designed the glass-topped vanity and lighting fixture for the house (opposite). The stool is a Danish design from the 1950s. The Holtons' bedroom (right) opens to the rear courtyard, which was originally enclosed by a wooden wall painted by Constantin Nivola. They preserved the mural with a new wall in front, and Nina added a geometric painting in Sert's favorite primary colors.

time-honored values

Long admired for his finely crafted furniture, Jens Risom belongs to the top tier of midcentury modern innovators. He is the last survivor of a group that included Charles Eames, George Nelson, and Eero Saarinen. "Eames and Saarinen were much more inventive with materials," admits the Danish-born octogenarian. "I set out to design contemporary furniture that was comfortable and practical to use." Instead of experimenting with plastics, he explored the most time-honored of materials—wood—to create an elegant, inviting style.

Although educated with Hans Wegner at the School of Arts and Crafts in Copenhagen, Risom does not consider himself a Danish designer. "I developed an American version of Scandinavian modern furniture," he explains. "It is more substantial than the light, thin-legged Danish designs."

In 1941, two years after he arrived in the United States, Risom began producing lines of furniture for Hans Knoll and Georg Jensen. The curving cypress frames of his first Knoll chairs were wrapped in olive green parachute webbing that failed to meet military standards. Risom formed Jens Risom Design in 1946 to manufacture and distribute his own furniture. In the late 1950s he began producing designs for the growing commercial market, including office and library furniture.

Risom's New Canaan dining room (above) features his own walnut dining table, chairs, and a hanging cabinet. Arne Jacobsen created the pendant light fixture in the 1950s for Poulsen. Apart from Jacobsen's 1958 Egg chair and a Danish sewing table, Risom's living room (right) is filled with his designs: a modular sofa, walnut tables and chairs, a round cherry coffee table with a travertine top, and webbed maple armchairs designed for Knoll in 1997.

The fruits of Risom's long career are best appreciated in his homes. For more than fifty years, the designer has lived in New Canaan, Connecticut—a mecca of midcentury modern houses by Marcel Breuer, Eliot Noyes, and Philip Johnson, whose 1949 glass house is the most famous. Risom lived in a New England–style 1950s house until 1999, when he moved to a smaller, one-story residence. Crowded with his wood-framed sofas, chairs, and tables, every space in the house showcases the range of his talents. Color in the whitewashed rooms is concentrated in the furniture's muted upholstery and abstract paintings and Scandinavian ceramics. Arne Jacobsen's Egg and Swan chairs, designed in 1958 for the SAS Royal Hotel in Copenhagen, pay homage to his Danish roots.

Risom's bedroom (left) is furnished with a Risom-designed platform bed with a hanging caned headboard. He also designed the red-cushioned laminated walnut chair in the late 1950s and the webbed chairs for Knoll in 1941. On his round table is Danish Saxbo pottery. As can be seen on the crowded drafting table in his study (below), Risom works at home on furniture designs, including a new table for his own dining room.

In his Block Island prefabricated house, the dining area (opposite) is defined by an oak table specially made by Risom for the space, surrounded by stacking chairs from his 1960s library series. Risom's slatted-back sofa (above) was custom designed to convert into a bed. He created the three-legged coffee table in 1967 just for the house. The colorful hanging light fixtures are Scandinavian.

In 1967 Risom built a second home on Block Island in Rhode Island, which he recently gave to his children. The prefabricated wooden cottage, raised on a deck and customized with heavier timbers, epitomizes his belief in simplicity. Completely sheathed in glass at both ends, its one-room interior is open to sea and sky. Lacquered pine floors and walls covered with barn siding provide a warm backdrop for groupings of Risom's furniture that subdivide the living spaces.

A 1967 article in *Life* magazine extolled the design's virtues, maintaining that it "bears as much resemblance to old-time prefab houses as today's sophisticated frozen foods do to what was available a few years ago." More than three decades later, *House and Garden* held up Risom's island retreat as a model for the future, noting its relevance to "how, entering a new millennium, we think about home and the life of a house."

mainstream modern: affordable style

It took a war—World War II—to move modernism into the mainstream. Despite the pioneering work of designers from Frank Lloyd Wright to Walter Gropius and Richard Neutra, modern ideas of what a home should be captured the public imagination only after synthetic materials, standardized parts, and prefabricated structures developed during the war paved the way.

Taking advantage of these technological advances, real estate developers such as William Levitt of the famed Levittowns ventured into mass-produced housing for wartime workers. Once the war was over in 1945, developers applied many of the same construction techniques to meet the demand of returning G.I.s and their families for inexpensive homes. Surging suburban populations led some builders—Robert Davenport in Virginia, Joseph Eichler in California, and Edward Hawkins in Colorado, for example—to experiment with flat roofs, asymmetrical facades, and open plans. Modernize your home, they told the public, and your life will become as up-to-date.

Museum exhibitions and publications also got the message out. From 1950 to 1955 the Museum of Modern Art in New York City held a series of bi-annual *Good Design* exhibitions in collaboration with the Merchandise Mart of Chicago. The shows influenced domestic taste, but just as important they stimulated progressive designers. The Triennale design exhibitions held in Milan during the 1950s assumed a similar role in Europe, particularly in showcasing the latest developments from Scandinavia.

Soon department stores began selling the "good design" of leading modernists, including T. H. Robsjohn-Gibbings, Paul McCobb, and Eva Zeisel. McCobb's modular furniture was featured in fifteen room settings at Bloomingdale's in New York in 1957. Magazines and books also helped promote the new look, often with the fervor of converts. In 1945 John Entenza, editor of the California-based *Arts + Architecture* magazine, launched a program to generate experimental steel-and-glass houses that he hoped would persuade builders and manufacturers to follow suit.

Although these modern designs never fully took hold in the marketplace, many of the ideas pioneered by Entenza, Eichler, and others can be found today in the average home. Open living areas, family rooms, eat-in kitchens, and an easy flow between indoors and out are all hallmarks of suburban houses a half century later.

Typical postwar furnishings fill this suburban sitting room: sofas modeled after 1950s designs by Edward Wormley, a 1949 Heywood-Wakefield coffee table, even a fiberglass California Kimball planter next to Philco's 1960 Predicta television. André Boratko's 1941 watercolor *Surreal Bird* hangs over the ensemble.

missionary living

CASE STUDY HOUSES NOS. 9, 16, AND 22 BY CHARLES EAMES AND EERO
SAARINEN, CRAIG ELLWOOD, AND PIERRE KOENIG · LOS ANGELES · 1945–59

The push for modern living assumed a missionary zeal when John Entenza, editor and publisher of the Los Angeles–based *Arts + Architecture* magazine, instituted the Case Study House program in 1945. Entenza's idea was to demonstrate that experimental housing could be just as comfortable and affordable as the traditional cottages of Levittown and other postwar suburbs. He offered architects the opportunity to design prototypical homes in unconventional materials with discounts from building product manufacturers. Southern California proved to be fertile ground.

Most of the selected architects—Charles Eames, Eero Saarinen, Craig Ellwood, Pierre Koenig, and Ralph Rapson, among others—were young and eager to take up Entenza's cause. They used off-the-shelf components and synthetic materials to create one-story, flat-roofed structures based on European concepts of flowing, open spaces. Not every project was built, but they were all published in the magazine.

The Case Study Houses generated great enthusiasm: the first six of the thirty-six houses designed were visited by nearly 400,000 people when they were unveiled in 1946–47. But the crisp, exacting architecture never caught on with the home-building industry, and—except for the house designed by Charles and Ray Eames (see pages 100–105)—the projects received little national publicity in their day.

John Entenza's own Case Study House, no. 9, designed by Eames and Saarinen, was restored in 1991 by the architect Barry Berkus as guest quarters and entertainment space and linked to a larger new house by a breezeway. Furnished with Saarinen's Womb chair and pedestal table, the living room's patio level includes a conversation corner behind a red-hot freestanding fireplace.

As a crusader for modern design, Entenza practiced what he preached. In 1945 the magazine editor tapped Charles Eames and Eero Saarinen to design Case Study House no. 9 as his own house on a bluff overlooking the Pacific Ocean in Pacific Palisades. Using the same steel components applied to the Eames House next door to Entenza's lot, the architects designed a steel-framed box punctuated by brightly colored panels.

In contrast to the exposed steel construction of the Eameses' two-story house and studio, Entenza's structure is largely concealed. Inside the one-story house, completed in 1949, the steel frame and all but one of four columns are covered by a wood-paneled ceiling and plaster walls. Private spaces such as bedrooms, a bathroom, and a study are sequestered on the side of the house nearest the road. The living room is divided into lower and upper sections and fronts a patio through a sliding-glass wall. It incorporates a sunken conversation corner with a built-in, wraparound sofa. On the carpeted upper level, a sliding door in the bedroom opens to a view across the living room and through the glass wall toward the ocean.

Sparsely furnished, the newly restored interiors feature the same contrasting colors as the exteriors. In the living area, a freestanding fireplace painted a vibrant orange-red, a tangerine sofa, and plywood Eames chairs stand out against the beige carpet, linen sofa upholstery, and plaster walls. Entenza also incorporated the latest gadgetry into his bachelor pad: movie projection facilities and hi-fi equipment built into the walls.

In the upper tier of the Entenza living room (above) are original hi-fi equipment and furniture by Eames, the house's co-designer, including a Soft Pad leather sofa, a lounge chair, and an Elliptical table. The view from the carport (right) reveals the geometric-patterned cement board. A built-in sofa in the living room's upper level (opposite) wraps around an Eames plywood table. The door leads to the bedroom.

The first of Craig Ellwood's three Case Study Houses, no. 16, was designed in 1952 for a site with spectacular views from the Bel Air hills. His most unusual idea for the steel-and-glass house was to enclose the interior spaces with floating screens rather than floor-to-ceiling partitions. The planes are finished in fir siding to provide a warm counterpoint to the painted steel. The same treatment is achieved outside in panels of translucent glass that protect the two bedrooms' outdoor courtyards from the street. Illuminated at night, the walls are transformed into shimmering planes of light.

Except for replacing the concrete flooring with tile, the owner has maintained all the original features. Japanese in feeling, the house is the ultimate expression of structural lightness and indoor-outdoor living promoted by the Case Study program. "I was never tied to standard detailing or inhibited from trying out new methods," recalled Ellwood, who was trained as an engineer. "When you haven't been taught that some detail is impossible, you approach it with confidence and innocence."

Like many architects in the Case Study program, Craig Ellwood framed his house no. 16 in steel and oriented the glass-enclosed main spaces to capture the best views. The house is a series of planes projecting into the landscape, its roof extending over the glass-enclosed dining room (far left) to adjoin the steel canopy shading the patio. Translucent glass panels (inset left) provide privacy by screening the bedroom courtyards from the street.

The living room of Ellwood's Case Study House no. 16 (above) is anchored by a stone fireplace whose chimney is shared with an outdoor barbecue. The Noguchi table was made by Herman Miller from 1948 to 1973. Built-in cabinets (right) separate the living and dining areas. Original appliances remain in the kitchen (left), which is set off from the dining room by a freestanding partition. The metal gate leads to a rear terrace.

"A man of steel" is the best way to describe the Case Study architect Pierre Koenig. For more than half a century, he has designed almost all his buildings in this durable metal. "Some of the cleanest and most immaculate thinking in the development of the small contemporary house," raved *Arts + Architecture* about his 1958 Case Study House no. 21. Built of simply detailed manufactured components, the steel-framed pavilion is surrounded by reflecting pools and illustrates a powerful dialogue between industry and nature.

Koenig's second Case Study House, no. 22, became even more famous than his first. In 1959 he was commissioned by C. H. (Buck) Stahl, a purchasing agent for Hughes Aircraft, and his wife, Carlotta, who had a lot in the Hollywood hills high above Sunset Boulevard. The Stahls wanted a glass house that would offer dramatic panoramas of Los Angeles. Buck Stahl went so far as to flatten the property's edge with his Cadillac to add a six-foot concrete promontory.

The architect complied with the Stahls' request by cantilevering the house over the cliff, supporting his prefabricated steel frame on concrete caissons. Almost totally enclosed in glass, the aerie rivals Mies van der Rohe's Farnsworth House in its minimalism. Inside the L-shaped structure, Koenig placed bedrooms and bathrooms against the solid street facade to allow the living areas to face out toward the swimming pool and views.

As the view from Koenig's Case Study House no. 22 has grown with the city, this house of glass has been up to the task. The glass-enclosed living room cantilevers over the hillside to take in a panoramic view of Los Angeles. A seven-foot-wide roof overhang shades the interior and an adjacent terrace, with its 1950s Van Keppel–Green chaise. Inside is George Nelson's 1955 Coconut chair.

In Case Study House no. 22, the owners put wood in place of the aluminum slats in the kitchen ceiling and refinished the mahogany-veneered cabinets flanking the dining room (inset right). Mysterious at night, the living room (far right) is furnished with an Eames lounge chair and Elliptical and wire-base tables. Under original ball lights, Nelson's Coconut chair is next to a 1950s floor lamp.

Completed in 1960, the house—still owned by the Stahls—instantly became a symbol of the contemporary California lifestyle. Its most celebrated image is Julius Shulman's night-time photograph of the glassy living room hovering over the glittering grid of streets below (see page 2). Like the houses that Entenza and Eames built for themselves, Case Study House no. 22 is classified as a Los Angeles city landmark. "We can change the interiors," says Carlotta Stahl, "but not the exterior."

Because building contractors regarded steel construction as too demanding of skilled labor, Koenig's design and other Case Study prototypes became influential as exemplars of casual, indoor-outdoor living rather than as actual models for suburban housing. These innovative houses did, however, become a source of inspiration for architects, particularly British high-tech designers in the 1960s. The last Case Study prototype, an apartment building in Newport Beach, California, was designed in 1964 but never realized, and the program was dropped. Today these low-slung, steel-framed houses are being sought after and restored as the landmarks they always have been.

symphony in steel

Screened by eucalyptus trees, Charles and Ray Eames's house and studio (below) are connected by a wooden walkway. The shoji-like steel frames filled with glass and colored panels reappeared in their 1950 modular storage units for Herman Miller (below right). The two-story studio (opposite), outfitted with a 1956 Eames lounge chair and ottoman, is framed by exposed steel frames, trusses, and roof decking.

The most famous and influential of all the Case Study Houses is no. 8, the steel-framed complex in Pacific Palisades, California, where the inventive husband-and-wife team of Ray and Charles Eames made their home. Divided into separate pavilions for living and work, the paired structures nestled against a hill epitomize the progressive goals of Entenza's Case Study Houses and the Eameses' interest in mass-produced design.

By 1945, when they published their first proposal for the house in *Arts + Architecture,* the couple had already produced lightweight, molded-plywood chairs, cabinets, and tables with technology developed for the military. They approached their house with the same industrial sensibility, ordering steel beams, columns, and trusses from a manufacturer's catalogue. The design evolved from an earlier bridge scheme conceived with Eero Saarinen to complement John Entenza's house (see pages 88–91).

Although matter-of-fact, the kit-of-parts construction is manipulated into an architecture of sophisticated beauty. Translucent glass, jalousie windows, and cement-board panels painted in white, gray, black, red, and blue fill the steel frames, lifted into place in just over a day. The crisply outlined, patterned facades resemble the rhythmic, linear paintings of the Dutch artist Piet Mondrian and Japanese shoji screens. (The Japanese association seems intentional: early photographs of the house show the main living space furnished solely with tatami mats, pillows, and Isamu Noguchi lamps.) On Christmas Eve 1949, the Eameses finally moved into their new home.

Off the entrance hallway in the Eames House, a steel-and-wood staircase (above) leads to the bedroom mezzanine. The double-height living area (right) is filled with the Eameses' furniture, from their Sofa Compact prototype and steel shelving to their folk-art collection. George Nelson's Bubble lamp is from 1947. Original open-weave drapes at the windows still screen out the sun.

The Eameses' mezzanine bedroom (left) gave them an ocean view from the balcony overlooking their living area. The couple's fiberglass armchair, designed in 1948, was manufactured by Herman Miller from 1950 to 1989. Japanese-style sliding panels (above) could be closed for privacy. Another sliding door between the master and guest bedrooms separated the sleeping areas.

The interiors of the Eames complex reflect the same ingenuity as its outer shell. Dominating the 1,500-square-foot house is an open, two-story living room that adjoins a kitchen and dining room placed under a second-floor sleeping loft. Separated by a courtyard, the 1,000-square-foot studio mirrors the house with a two-story workroom and a darkroom and bathroom tucked under a mezzanine. The steel structure is left exposed throughout, but unpainted canvas covers cement-board panels inside. Banks of windows invite in views and form a subtle boundary between indoors and out.

The Eameses humanized their spaces with wood paneling, furnishings of their own design, and ample evidence of their creative, inquisitive lives. Cluttering every surface were treasures collected from the couple's travels: Mexican dolls, Japanese combs, pre-Columbian artifacts, woven boxes, toy trains, rocks, and sticks. Seating was covered with colorful weavings and pillows. Artwork—a Hans Hofmann painting given by Entenza, a weathervane from Billy Wilder, and Herbert Matter photography—testified to long-standing friendships.

Lucia Eames, Charles's only child, now owns the complex, which remains much as it looked when Ray died in 1988, ten years after Charles. "We are fortunate enough to use it as the family homestead," explains grandson Eames Demetrios, who works in the studio producing videos, films, and CD-ROMs for the Eames Office. The heirs have done little to change the house and studio except to make repairs, such as replacing dozens of glass panes after the 1994 earthquake. "We want to make sure the house survives," says Demetrios. "But we don't want to cover it with Saran Wrap." Keeping this airy, serene domain alive seems to be just what Ray and Charles Eames intended.

suburban frontier

EUGENE STERNBERG AND JOSEPH DION · ENGLEWOOD, COLORADO · 1949–57

"The best house you could get after the war was a box," says the World War II veteran Michael Freed. But Freed and his wife, Sylvia, discovered an exciting alternative when they visited a Denver home show in 1950. On display was a model house from a new subdivision in Arapahoe County just south of the city. "It had architecture. It had style," says Freed. "We couldn't wait to find the developer."

That developer turned out to be Edward Hawkins, a builder and self-taught designer who was marketing Arapahoe Acres. Hawkins based his modern, low-slung homes on the architecture of Frank Lloyd Wright, and he set them on broad, curved streets and sweeping lawns planted to retain mountain vistas. Plans for the thirty-acre community began in 1949 after Hawkins tapped Eugene Sternberg, a Czech-born architect who had worked in London, to design the first nine houses using a single, four-square layout. All of them sold immediately.

Life magazine called Sternberg's design one of the "best houses under $15,000." *Better Homes and Gardens* sold a complete set of his plans for $25. Success led Hawkins to increase his prices and replace Sternberg, who strongly advocated low-cost housing, with one of the architect's students, Joseph Dion. The new houses were larger, more luxurious, and drew on Wright's Usonian style, with horizontal lines and earthy colors.

The 124 houses of Arapahoe Acres still stand as a testament to Hawkins's vision. "The neighborhood is remarkably well preserved," says Debby Pool, who moved here with her husband, Dick, in 1955. Preserved with covenants and an architectural review committee, the suburb was named a national historic district in 1998. The Pools, Freeds, and other pioneers remember how Hawkins, who resided here until 1966, sold them on his ideas. "He really believed in this community," recalls Pool. "How many developers do you know who live in the neighborhoods they construct?"

Some of the first homes in Arapahoe Acres were placed atop the highest point, while others were tucked into the hillside—allowing varied layouts. Preservationist Diane Wray, who has written a history of the community, furnished her home with classics such as Harry Bertoia's 1952 Bird chair and ottoman (below). Phil and Florine Boxer also turned to Bertoia, using a quartet of his 1952 Diamond chairs (opposite).

into the woods

CHARLES GOODMAN · ALEXANDRIA, VIRGINIA · 1949–60S

Driving through Hollin Hills on a summer afternoon, it is hard to see the houses for the trees. The leafy, 225-acre subdivision in Alexandria, Virginia, a few miles south of Washington, D.C., was planned to respect the natural beauty of its wooded hills. In creating this pioneering community—one of the few Washington suburbs noted for its modern architecture—the developer Robert Davenport and the architect Charles Goodman shunned features typical of postwar suburbs. They eliminated sidewalks, uniform front lawns, and backyard fences. They set aside thirty acres of open space for parks and a community center, and they sited the houses on different-size lots to maximize privacy and views.

From 1949 on, each house was sold with a landscape plan for an additional $100, which included a consultation with the landscape architect Lou Bernard Voight. (After Voight died in 1953, Dan Kiley took his place.) Extending this environmental sensitivity to the house designs, Goodman developed a cost-effective, modular construction system of wood and glass that allowed for expansion and variation. When faced with a sloping lot, for example, the architect added a second level to his one-story model so that bedrooms, recreation room, and bathroom could be tucked into the low side of the hill. Walls and chimneys of recycled brick and low gabled roofs made them look like they could "slide through the trees," according to Goodman.

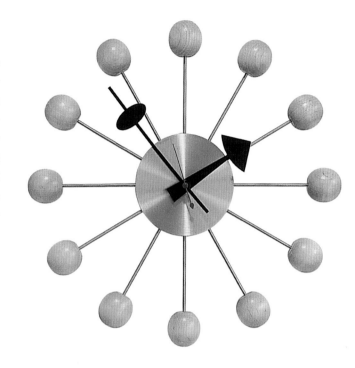

Barbara Boyd and Ron Marshall's sitting room (opposite) features a Bertoia chair, a Heywood-Wakefield table, a sofa with 1950s fabric, and an Eames screen. In the original living room (right), period treasures include 1950s Kroehler chairs, a bench from Paul McCobb's Planner Group, vases by Fratelli Toso and Venini, a Lightolier floor lamp, and a 1950s fan. George Nelson's 1950 ball clock still tells time in the foyer (above).

The couple's dining room (opposite) is furnished with a table, chairs, and buffet all from Heywood-Wakefield. Shelves hold 1950s ceramics by Gunnar Nylund and Dutch Gouda vases. Arrayed on a McCobb Planner Group cabinet is a collection of Nordic pots (left). Practicality reigns in the kitchen (above left), with its reproduction 1950s chrome dining set. On the terrace (above right) is early 1960s furniture made by Hillcrest.

111

Buyers could add extras, upgrading asphalt-tile floors to brick, hardwood, or slate; selecting exterior and interior paneling; and choosing built-in furnishings. Because Washington had few stores offering cutting-edge furniture, Davenport sold Knoll products and had local suppliers outfit his model homes with the latest Hans Wegner, Eero Saarinen, and Charles and Ray Eames designs.

In 1952 Goodman inverted the standard roof pitch to a chevron-shaped butterfly style to provide cathedral ceilings inside. One of his most radical designs was a flat-topped box with the bathroom, laundry, and closets clustered at the center. *House and Home* magazine in 1954 dubbed it "the most advanced builder house in the U.S." By the early 1960s Goodman had invented fifteen unit types from his original formula. Almost as soon as the houses were built, they were expanded. Few houses remain in original condition, although additions are usually sympathetic because an architectural review committee scrutinizes all building plans.

Barbara Boyd and Ron Marshall, who both work at the U.S. Department of Defense, bought a 1968 house in Hollin Hills based on a 1950s Goodman design to showcase their collection of midcentury modern furniture and accessories. "We only do blond," laughs Boyd, pointing to a Heywood-Wakefield desk and a Paul McCobb table. Upholstered in jellybean colors of pink, yellow, and aqua, the furniture is accented by black pieces such as the living room's plywood Eames chair and fireplace screen and andirons designed by Donald Deskey. Nearly every item in the house—from plates and glasses to the living room fan and the television in the spacious studio added by the previous owner—is a postwar original.

Midcentury design has become the couple's passion, and the two spend most of their vacations scouting furniture shows and flea markets for new finds. During recent trips to Stockholm and Copenhagen, they purchased ceramic pots by noted postwar Scandinavian designers such as Gunnar Nylund, Stig Lindberg, and Carl-Harry Stalhane, among others. "We are each other's conscience," says Boyd in discussing their shopping trips. Adds Marshall: "I always ask, Where are we going to put it?"

A lamp in the guest bedroom (above) was made by Royal Haeger. Reflected in the mirror is a 1937 Heywood-Wakefield bed and a 1940s fan from Fresh'nd-Aire. The owners' bedroom has a 1949–51 ash suite by Ernest Herrman for Heywood Wakefield. A 1950s French starburst mirror hangs above a Heywood-Wakefield table-desk in the foyer (opposite). Per Lutken designed the glass vessels in 1957 for Holmegaard.

Based on site and functional requirements, houses throughout Hollin Hills are variations on a number of basic unit types. Selected examples include (top to bottom) a flat-roofed box based on unit type five, a gabled version of unit type eight, a butterfly-roof house based on unit type six with a brick addition, and a rectilinear house designed by Cass Neer in 1958 in the spirit of Charles Goodman's originals. Barbara Boyd and Ron Marshall's house (opposite) was completed in 1968 according to Goodman's modified unit type seven.

umbrella in the sun

PAUL RUDOLPH · SARASOTA, FLORIDA · 1953

A resort town on the Gulf of Mexico seems an unlikely place to set design trends. But in the late 1940s and the 1950s, Sarasota, Florida, became a hotbed of new ideas, fueled by speculative development and moneyed vacationers. Here architects mirrored the modernism promoted by the California Case Study Houses and tempered it to the tropics.

Houses were constructed of native materials such as cypress and concrete block and raised on stilts above the watery ground. Overhanging roofs, louvered walls, and shutters shaded their open spaces from strong sunlight. Jalousie windows and sliding doors promoted ventilation. Screened courtyards kept away the bugs.

This regional modernism was adopted by a group of local architects known as the Sarasota School, who came to share a vision first articulated by Ralph Twitchell and Paul Rudolph. The two architects pioneered a climate-sensitive modernism through new technologies such as curved, catenary roofs, plastic paneling, and marine plywood. "They were able to experiment more than the architects of the Case Study Houses because they were designing second homes for wealthy people from the Midwest and Northeast," explains the Tampa architect John Howey, author of a 1995 book on the Sarasota School.

For this house in Sarasota, now owned by Gary and Carol Stover, Rudolph flanked the double-height living room at its center with banks of jalousie windows to admit breezes. The two-story wood-slatted "umbrella" that originally extended over the house and pool was destroyed in a hurricane. Only a remnant of the trellis remains over the roof.

The Stovers repainted the living room (opposite) in original colors and re-upholstered George Nelson's 1952 modular seating left by the previous owners. The stairway and bridge connecting second-story bedrooms shelters a sunken seating area with a 1950s bench and a Russel Wright torchère. The boxy shelf overhanging the second level (below) is the back of built-in drawers.

Progressive real estate developers promoted their innovations. One of the most prominent was Philip Hiss, who in the early 1950s built a waterfront colony of speculative houses named Lido Shores. The most extraordinary of these model homes—Hiss designed several himself—was created in 1953 by Rudolph, who had studied at Harvard University under the Bauhaus master Walter Gropius. Shading the entire two-story structure was an "umbrella": a huge wood-slatted trellis that extended from the front of the house to the back. It surrounded the terrace and swimming pool, forming a protective shield over the house's lower roof.

In 1997 the retired Wall Street consultants Gary and Carol Stover purchased Rudolph's Umbrella House and have since restored it. With the advice of Howey and the benefit of the original drawings, they upgraded the kitchen and bathrooms and repainted the rooms in their original gray and buff colors. Gary took to heart the task of researching the house and nominated it to the National Register of Historic Places.

The Stovers have also begun to collect period furniture. They began by reupholstering a George Nelson sofa and chair left by the previous owners and then scouted antiques markets for pieces by Russel Wright, Carl Jacobs, and Kurt Versen. The couple bought a set of Harry Bertoia chairs from Howey and even managed to find a desk from another Rudolph house for the ground-floor study. "We've tried to stay with the original look without overwhelming the architecture," says Carol.

One part of the house that the Stovers have not reinstated, however, is Rudolph's umbrella. The monumental canopy was destroyed by a hurricane in the 1960s and never resurrected. "It would be nice to put it back," says Gary. "But it presents many challenges in terms of current building codes. Right now, we like the house the way it is."

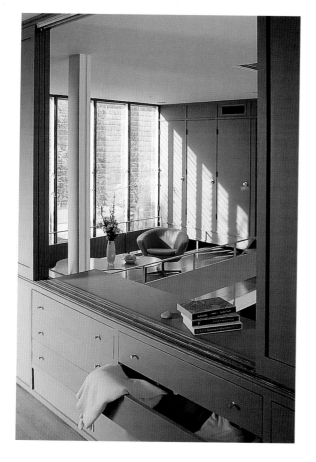

The dining area, seen from the second level (opposite), is furnished with Bertoia steel-wire chairs. The bedroom (above left) opens onto the double-height living room through a sliding door above built-in drawers that form an abstract ledge (left). On the stair landing (above right), Swedish items—1950s swivel chairs by Overman and a lamp by Kurt Versen—are next to an anonymous biomorphic coffee table.

western pioneers

No one did more to make the modern house accessible to the average home buyer than the real estate developer Joseph Eichler. From 1949 to 1968, Eichler produced more than twelve thousand California houses that were affordable yet had the look of custom architecture. These wood-framed residences, built primarily in the Bay Area, epitomize the postwar dream house with clean, simple lines and large expanses of glass that open to planted courtyards and patios.

Eichler attributed his passion for modern design to renting Frank Lloyd Wright's Bazett House (1939) on the San Francisco peninsula in the early 1940s. After building several conventional tract houses in 1947, the developer embarked on a more experimental direction. In 1949 he hired Robert Anshen of Anshen and Allen in San Francisco to draw up plans for a three-bedroom, one-bathroom, 900-square-foot house in Sunnyvale, near San Jose. The prototype featured what would become the Eichler signature: post-and-beam construction and modular panels of redwood and glass. Inside, kitchens opened to family rooms with floor-to-ceiling glass. Priced at $9,500 each, all fifty models sold within two weeks.

From its unassuming entrance leading to a landscaped atrium (above and left), this 1956 Eichler house owned by Ron Crider and Jeffrey Friedman illustrates the developer's emphasis on indoor-outdoor living. The living room (opposite) is furnished with vintage Bertoia Diamond chairs, paired with a Noguchi coffee table. George Nelson designed both the slatted bench and the Sunburst clock, while the rug is a reissue of a 1920s Eileen Gray design.

More midcentury finds are in the family room (opposite): a Nelson Coconut chair, a Florence Knoll sofa and marble-topped table, an Eames Elliptical table, a Sidney Gordin sculpture, Danish glass, and *Solitude* (1946) by Leah Rinne Hamilton. In the living room (above) are a 1958 Vladimir Kagan sofa, a 1949 Gino Sarfatti light fixture, and a 1949 Nelson cabinet. Saarinen Womb chairs and ottomans (right) occupy the library.

Eichler continued to experiment with his subdivisions in the 1950s. Streets were arranged in concentric circles and cul-de-sacs, and community centers were built with swimming pools. House designs grew more sophisticated, featuring separate bedroom areas for parents and children, additional bathrooms, built-in furniture, and laundry rooms. Landscaped atriums were added to the center of the houses to make nature part of everyday living. By 1959 Eichler Homes was producing seven hundred houses a year and in 1960 expanded from the Bay Area to Los Angeles. Eichler also pioneered in establishing integrated neighborhoods. He sold houses to Asians and African Americans at a time when the government still endorsed restrictive covenants.

"Eichlers" are still popular today, fetching prices as high as $1 million. Their primary appeal is the same as it was in the 1950s: sunny spaces that are connected to the outdoors. "The flow of the rooms and glass walls give a feeling of openness," says Ron Crider, the proud owner of a 1956 Eichler house in San Mateo's Highlands community. "From every vantage point, you feel like you are communing with nature." After buying the four-bedroom house in 1995, Crider and his partner, Jeffrey Friedman, undertook minor modernizations, installing ceramic tile in the main living areas. "The bones were intact," notes Crider, who adds that the original radiant-heating system in the concrete floor "still works beautifully."

Designed by Jones and Emmons of Los Angeles, the house inspired the pair to upgrade their collection of midcentury modern furnishings from 1950s kitsch to classics. They recently replaced a 1940s dining room set with a Florence Knoll table, Eero Saarinen chairs, and a George Nelson wall cabinet. In the living room, Harry Bertoia's Diamond chairs are paired with a curvaceous sofa by Vladimir Kagan and a glass-topped coffee table by Isamu Noguchi. Crider has also amassed an impressive collection of abstract artworks of the period by West Coast artists such as Charles Green Shaw and Burgoyne Diller.

Owners such as Crider and Friedman now have the benefit of the Eichler Network, a quarterly newsletter and Web site that offers everything from community news to recommended renovation specialists. According to Crider, the network "is almost a cult."

A Knoll walnut table, Saarinen Naugahyde chairs, and a Nelson walnut Basic cabinet star in the dining room (opposite). In the cabinet is Eva Zeisel's Fantasy series for Hallcraft. Glass vases are by Tapio Wirkkala. The light fixture is a reproduction of a 1957 Poul Henningsen design. On the walls are works by the American Abstract Artists group and the Chicago Bauhaus artist Daniel Massen. Original wood cabinets and ball lights remain in the kitchen (below).

passion for plastic

RALPH WILSON SR. AND BONNIE MCININICH · TEMPLE, TEXAS · 1959

No materials symbolize the postwar era better than chemically based synthetics. The most popular was applied to tables and countertops—plastic laminate, which was developed in 1909 to encase electrical wiring and then adapted as a decorative veneer. Plastic laminate, commonly called Formica after one of its leading producers, grew increasingly more sophisticated as a durable, easily cleaned finish. By the mid-1950s a dozen American companies were manufacturing laminates for use in the kitchen and bathroom.

Covering tabletops and counters, however, was not enough for Ralph Wilson Sr., who founded Wilsonart International in 1956. In 1959 Wilson set out to persuade the public that plastics were as durable and beautiful as wood, tile, linoleum, and other traditional finishes. He and his daughter Bonnie McIninich designed and built a 3,000-square-foot home in Temple, Texas, as a company showcase.

Virtually every surface of the one-story, U-shaped house is decorated in Wilsonart products. Kitchen and bathroom cabinets, counters (including one of the earliest continuous-curve, or postformed, laminates), and even the shower stall are sheathed in bright colors, metallic flecks, and wood-grain patterns. Instead of plasterboard, many of the walls bear laminate panels applied directly to wood framing.

Although Formica similarly demonstrated its products at the 1964 World's Fair, Wilson's house was the domestic pioneer. Promoted in company advertisements and trade magazines, the house became living proof of plastic's versatility. Wilson actually lived in the house until his death in 1972. In this laboratory, he experimented with different decorations in the main rooms and lined the open-air garage with new wood-grain products to test their weather resistance.

A pair of Jens Risom armchairs sits next to nesting tables and a glass coffee table by Poul Kjaerholm. Curves in the reproduction Eames lounge chair are echoed in a vintage Saarinen Womb chair and Bertoia Diamond chairs on the terrace. The Sunburst clock is another playful design by George Nelson.

128

In 1996 Wilson's widow, Sunny, put the house up for sale and began remodeling the interior until the company archivist Grace Jeffers stepped in to save it from destruction. A New York–based decorative arts historian and daughter of a Formica salesman, Jeffers—who has been dubbed the "Dalai Laminate"—instantly recognized the house's historical importance.

"When I walked in, I absolutely flipped out," she says. "Here plastic laminates were being used in innovative ways that most people would date to the mid-1960s." Jeffers persuaded Wilsonart to renovate the house and its garden as a museum. The open-plan spaces, now filled with vintage and reproduction 1950s pieces, testify to the design potential of this modest sandwich of melamine- and phenolic-treated materials.

Venini glass pendant fixtures in the restored Wilson House are suspended over George Nelson's 1946 gateleg dining table and chairs (above). The melamine bowls atop the table are from the 1950s, and the upholstered chair is by Poul Dinesen. The kitchen (opposite top) features original appliances and, of course, a salad of colorful plastic laminates, which also cover nearly every surface of the bathroom (opposite bottom).

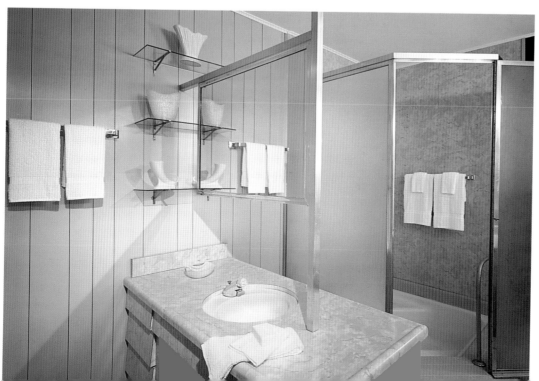

back to the future:
living with midcentury modern

Once relegated to basements and junk shops, midcentury modern furniture is back in style. Vintage designs by the Eameses, Eero Saarinen, and Arne Jacobsen are now as sought after—and nearly as pricey—as centuries-old antiques. Manufacturers such as Herman Miller and Knoll have put 1940s and 1950s designs by the Eameses, George Nelson, and Jens Risom back into production, and even tradition-oriented Baker Furniture is reproducing a line by the Danish designer Finn Juhl. Museums have added their prestige with recent exhibits focused on postwar modern design and architecture.

Collecting modern furniture began in the 1980s as a reaction against the ornamented decor popular at the time. It took root with casual foraging for 1950s flea-market kitsch but blossomed in the 1990s into connoisseurship. Enthusiasm for postwar artifacts soon spawned numerous stores, galleries, publications, and Web sites specializing in modern design.

Clean-lined and simple, midcentury furnishings are appealing as symbols of an era when confidence and optimism about the future reigned. Their popularity as collectibles has led to a serious reappraisal of postwar design around the world. Appreciation for manufactured furnishings by Americans such as Eero Saarinen, Isamu Noguchi, and Paul McCobb has been followed by an interest in rarer, one-of-a-kind designs by Serge Mouille, Jean Prouvé, Gio Ponti, and other Europeans. Scandinavian modern design in particular—wood furniture, glass, and ceramics—is enjoying a rebirth as a finely crafted alternative to metal, plywood, and plastic furniture. Some of these once-affordable tokens of good design have now entered the rarefied realm of antiquarianism.

A San Diego collector found the perfect home for her midcentury modern furnishings when she came upon this 1960 house of glass by the noted architect Richard Neutra. Pierre Paulin's Slice chair and the Eameses' Elliptical coffee table add curvaceous, colorful contrasts to the living room's rectilinear lines.

Collecting midcentury modern furnishings has fueled a renewed interest in domestic architecture of the period. Today's serious collectors like to buy not only the furniture but the house to go with it. They are restoring high-style homes designed by leading modernists such as Richard Neutra as well as developer-built progeny. Many owners have gone so far as to safeguard their midcentury properties—and entire neighborhoods—by having them declared state and national historic landmarks. For baby boomers, many of these houses and their furnishings represent the surroundings of their youth, which may explain why they have become its most avid collectors.

the art of reduction

CLARENCE MAYHEW · OAKLAND, CALIFORNIA · 1960

Michael and Gabrielle Boyd have spent the past two decades amassing hundreds of pieces of modern furniture and artwork. Dating from the early 1900s to the 1960s, their collection reflects what they call "the art of reduction," the paring down of a design to its most essential ingredients.

Well represented among their treasures are the great figures of American midcentury design—Harry Bertoia, Charles and Ray Eames, George Nelson, Isamu Noguchi, Richard Neutra, and Eero Saarinen—as well as leading Europeans of the period such as Arne Jacobsen, Jean Prouvé, and Alexander Noll. The Boyds' collection is considered so significant that 150 pieces from it were exhibited at the San Francisco Museum of Modern Art in 1998.

But far from considering their furniture as precious artifacts, the Boyds and their two sons enjoy them as part of their everyday lives. They dine on red vinyl–covered chairs designed by the Italian architect Gio Ponti for a corporate headquarters in Milan. They check the time by looking at George Nelson's Ball clock. They relax in front of their fireplaces on a chair designed by Hans Wegner and ottomans by Frank Lloyd Wright.

In the living room (left) are an Eames screen and steel Storage Unit plus a wooden stool designed by Ray Eames. A Carlo Scarpa vase rests on a Mies table. Sculpted shapes in black leather include Arne Jacobsen's sofa and 1958 Swan chair and Hans Wegner's 1960 Ox chair (right). The Italian floor lamp is from Arteluce. Paintings include a Morris Louis (left) and Burgoyne Diller's *First Theme* (right). Frank Gehry did the snaking cardboard, Man Ray the bronze on the Eames Elliptical table.

The furnishings are installed in a 1960 ranch house near Oakland, California, designed by Clarence Mayhew, with a walled garden created by the noted landscape architect Lawrence Halprin. The Boyds purchased the home in 1996 and then hired the local architect Thom Faulders to remove elements added by previous owners—knotty pine, wagon wheels, and brass chandeliers—and open the living room to the library, which once displayed guns. "We called it the Gunsmoke look when we first moved in," notes Michael Boyd. White walls and black floors now set off original ceiling beams, wood paneling, and brick fireplaces, forming a spare backdrop to the couple's furnishings.

Boyd, who composes music for films and commercials, began collecting modern furniture in 1981. His first purchase was a 1950 Eames fiberglass chair, followed by Jacobsen's 1952 Ant chair. "Suddenly," he says, "I was swept away." In 1989 he married Gabrielle, who now runs his business, and the two continued their obsessive search for minimalist objects. In researching their purchases, the Boyds started another collection—a library of design books.

Michael Boyd says that he is "fascinated by the notion that a chair or a piece of functional design suggests the architecture and sense of space of its creator." By way of example, he points to the similarities between the steel-framed home designed by Charles and Ray Eames and the Eameses' famous Storage Unit in his living room (see page 100).

The Boyds continue to collect "at a heavy pace," but not every item among their holdings is well worn or displayed. Rare items, such as Nelson's Marshmallow sofa and Noguchi's chess table, are stashed in an upstairs sitting room. Others have been donated to the San Francisco Museum of Modern Art, where they are secure as part of its permanent design collection.

George Nelson's 1956 Marshmallow sofa in an upstairs sitting room is flanked by an Eames fiberglass chair and Marco Zanuso's 1951 Lady armchair. In front is Noguchi's classic coffee table, and above is Nelson's Bubble lamp. On the wall are modern works on paper, including a 1925 study for an Eileen Gray rug.

Around the Boyds' 1950s Baker table (left) are Gio Ponti chairs from 1936. Jean Prouvé, Charlotte Perriand, and Sonia Delaunay collaborated on the 1952 storage unit. Poul Henningsen did the chandelier; the sconce is from Arteluce. Entry treasures (above) include a Gerrit Rietveld chair and 1923 coat rack and an Eames Storage Unit topped by Walter Dorwin Teague's 1939 desk lamp.

Next to Frank Lloyd Wright's ottomans in the library (left) is a chaise by Le Corbusier and Charlotte Perriand; the steel-tube armchair is Mies's MR20 model. The book-laden table is an Eames prototype. In the family room (above) is an Eames cabinet and a Paulin chair. Art is by John McLaughlin (left) and Ilya Bolotowsky (above). On Breuer nesting tables (right) are a Henry Dreyfuss thermos and a lamp by Wilfred Bucquet.

minimalist temple

RICHARD NEUTRA · SAN DIEGO, CALIFORNIA · 1960

It did not take Susan Camiel long to decide to buy San Diego's last intact Richard Neutra house. "I was speechless for the first ten minutes," says Camiel after walking through the front door. "All I saw was floor-to-ceiling glass."

Perched on a clifftop overlooking Mission Valley, the modest 1960 home opens to a sweeping panorama at the rear through a bank of sliding-glass doors. A hallway between the transparent wall and the main rooms offers a view along the house's entire length. This open, boxcar arrangement is typical of the smaller houses designed by Neutra in the 1950s and 1960s.

Camiel, the house's third owner, instantly recognized its architectural pedigree. Since the mid-1980s she had purchased classic modern furnishings designed by Neutra's contemporaries from Boomerang for Modern in San Diego's Little Italy neighborhood. The store's owner, David Skelley, helped Camiel find the Neutra house in 1999 and reinstate its period look. "We see design from the same angle," notes Skelley. "When we put the house together, it was like one person doing it."

The house's birch paneling and built-in furniture were in mint condition, but the concrete-block fireplace had been concealed by mirrors and a fan. After removing these intrusions, Skelley painted the fireplace a gray green to make it stand out against the blond wood surfaces and oatmeal-colored carpet.

The terrace by the pool (above) offers a courtyard view. Neutra's son, Dion, designed the guest house (left and opposite) in the 1970s. It is now home to a Risom sofa, Bertoia Diamond chair, and Florence Knoll table. Camiel's mother, Laurie Blankfort-Raymond, created the sculpture on the table, and the Chicago artist Michael Higgins did the mobile. The rya rug is from the 1960s.

In furnishing the airy, neutral spaces, Camiel drew on her collection of architect-designed furniture and also installed newly acquired pieces. Pierre Paulin's purple Slice chair, Charles and Ray Eames's Elliptical coffee table, and Eero Saarinen's red Womb chair and ottoman join Neutra's blue built-in sofa in the living room. Behind this grouping, a door slides open to reveal the bedroom outfitted with Verner Panton's orange Cone chair, George Nelson's Thin Edge bed, and an Isamu Noguchi Akari lamp.

Camiel, who is hearing impaired, reflects that the house "has made me more social by bringing people into my life." She belongs to a group of midcentury modern "maniacs" who met through Skelley and now host monthly dinners at each other's homes. "This house brings pleasure to people, and I enjoy that," says Camiel. "I'm just the custodian of the architecture. It really belongs to the community."

Her guardianship of Neutra's legacy led San Diego to designate the house a historic landmark in 1999. "The house wasn't particularly distinguished when it was built," admits Dion Neutra, the architect's son. "Now it's important because it's the only Neutra house in the San Diego area that hasn't lost the historic flavor of the period."

Neutra's birch storage walls (opposite) and built-in sofa with its original Knoll fabric (left) frame the living room, with Saarinen's Womb chair and ottoman. A Blenko vase and a Danish teak bowl enliven the tabletop (above). Camiel credits her parents, the screenwriter Michael Blankfort and the artist Laurie Blankfort-Raymond—who created the painting on the far bedroom wall—with her interest in modern design.

Camiel's bedroom (right) contains a desk and shelving designed by Neutra, a stool from Saarinen's 1956 pedestal series, an Eames table, George Nelson's 1956 Thin Edge bed, Verner Panton's 1958 Cone chair, Isamu Noguchi's 1951 Japanese-inspired Akari floor lamp, and a Greta Grossman desk fixture. The abstract weaving in the bedroom hallway (below) is from IBM in Los Angeles.

calming effect

RICHARD NEUTRA · GLENDALE, CALIFORNIA · 1961

"I'm a purist," admits John Solomon, an executive at Walt Disney Imagineering, in describing his taste in furnishings and art. "Everything has to be vintage. I don't have any reproductions." Solomon prefers original 1940s and 1950s classics by George Nelson, Eero Saarinen, Isamu Noguchi, and Ray and Charles Eames. He even owns the experimental prototype for a mass-produced plywood coffee table designed by the Eameses in 1948. "It's like a study for a painting," he marvels.

For years, the Disney executive had searched for the perfect setting for his midcentury modern collection. He had almost given up when he called a real estate agent who suggested a visit to a 1961 house in Glendale, a few miles outside Los Angeles. Designed by Richard Neutra in the modest style typical of his late work, the two-bedroom, 1,700-square-foot home was still owned by the wife of the couple who commissioned it. For decades, they had immaculately maintained its original features, from the built-in wood cabinets down to the paint colors. In a matter of days, Solomon became the second owner of a modern house as pure as his furniture collection.

Solomon's flat-roofed house is nestled under a spreading live oak in a 1955 subdivision of Glendale, California, outside Los Angeles (left). Its open structure with a carport and the indoor-outdoor connection are hallmarks of Richard Neutra's style. Glass doors lead to the terrace. A Claes Oldenberg drawing hangs in the entrance foyer (right), which has a view into the living room.

An Eames lounge chair and plywood screen flank a Saarinen pedestal table in the library (above). Living room seating (right) includes Nelson's Coconut chair and Mies's Barcelona chair; the black leather sofa was custom made for the house by the original owners. On the sofa is a wrapped sculpture by Christo. The plywood coffee table is a 1948 prototype by Charles and Ray Eames.

Anchoring Solomon's living room (left) is a stacked brick fireplace, a Neutra signature. It is hung with a painting by Richard Artschwager. The hearth floats above the floor, allowing it to double as seating. George Nelson's 1954 pedestal table (right), whose white base contrasts with the wood drawers, stands in front of the master bedroom.

The property is located on a cul-de-sac in a 1955 subdivision built around huge live oaks. Neutra designed the flat-roofed house to accommodate two of the tall trees and oriented the rooms to vistas of the surrounding hillsides and mountains through large expanses of glass. "What I love about the house is a combination of glass, wood, and openness," says Solomon. He views his home as an uncluttered alternative to the crowded art-filled Manhattan apartment where he grew up as the son of the collector Horace Solomon and the art dealer Holly Solomon. "This style of architecture has a calming effect on me." Interior spaces underscore the inside-outside connection with few doors between rooms to interrupt the flow.

So as not to overpower Neutra's design, Solomon has furnished the rooms sparingly. His judiciously placed furniture is complemented by 1950s light fixtures and Scandinavian ceramics, which he admires for their unusual shapes and glazes. Not everything in the house reflects the postwar period, however. Paintings and sculptures by well-known artists of the 1960s such as Claes Oldenberg, Andy Warhol, and Christo punctuate the neutral spaces, along with more contemporary works.

Solomon, who produces films for Disney theme parks, considers his collection of modern art and design an extension of his creativity. At the end of a long day, he is happy to return to Neutra's light-filled spaces, to relax on the living room sofa or the patio under the shade of a spreading oak. "This house positively influences me," Solomon says. "It amplifies my creative spirit."

industrial evolution

JOHN LAWRENCE · NEW ORLEANS, LOUISIANA · 1958

Ronald Swartz, M.D., learned more than medicine during his 1970s residency at a New York City hospital. Combing junk stores and antiques shops in his spare time, he cultivated an abiding interest in twentieth-century furniture. "I started with American Art Deco," he says. "Back then, it was affordable." By 1984, when Swartz married Ellen Johnson, an arts publicist, his New Orleans house was stacked floor to ceiling with machine-age treasures.

Swartz and Johnson spent the next two years looking for larger quarters that would harmonize with the furniture. "Finding a modernist home in a city steeped in antiquities was not an easy task," says Johnson. They eventually discovered a 1958 house in Lake Vista, a postwar subdivision on Lake Pontchartrain, north of downtown New Orleans. Designed by John Lawrence, the former dean of Tulane University's architecture school, the one-story brick structure is "V-shaped for two-zone living," declared *House and Garden* in a 1960 feature on the house.

Past a metal fence, a gate, and a covered walkway, the door opens to a glassed-in passageway connecting two wings that fan out to shelter a landscaped courtyard bordered by paved terraces. Housed in the square block on the west side are living spaces, while to the east the narrower structure contains bedrooms, a study, and utility rooms. "We don't see anything but green space, and the neighbors reside just a few yards away," says Johnson, who works at home. "The architect was a genius in giving a feeling of both spaciousness and privacy."

As seen from the rear of the property (above), the house is divided into two wings housing living areas, at left, and bedrooms, at right. The living room (opposite) is bordered by a Nelson slatted bench, a Florence Knoll sofa, and an Aero-Art serving cart. Nestled into the corner are a 1954 Noguchi table, Bertoia steel-wire chairs, and a reproduction of a 1950s Serge Mouille lamp. Hanging next to the Art Deco chest is a painting salvaged from a dumpster in New York.

The living room's angular fireplace (left) is echoed in John Lawrence's travertine-topped coffee table. Around them are George Nelson's Swaged Leg fiberglass chairs, a round 1927 table by Donald Deskey, and a 1929 Paul Frankl chair. A Frankl table and chairs from the 1940s fill the dining room (above), with its anonymous cabinet as well as a WPA painting by Kenneth Bradley Loomis.

Streamlined Deco forms in the study (left) include a French desk and a 1928 Deskey table and 1930s chrome chairs. The Thonet desk chair from the 1950s is based on the Eames plywood classic. Tucked into a bedroom corner (below) is a walnut chest by George Nelson. In front of a slatted bench based on the Nelson classic, a 1929 Frankl sofa dominates the sitting room (right). Other finds are 1950s Italian lighting from Arteluce and, by a futuristic coffee table, William Lescaze's 1929 armchair.

After moving in, Swartz and Johnson undertook few renovations. The original wood paneling, plastic-laminate countertops, and travertine-trimmed fireplace were all intact. "We love the period and wanted to leave it alone," notes Swartz. The couple simply removed insensitive additions such as a built-in Queen Anne–style cabinet and chandeliers in the dining and breakfast rooms.

Living in the house has led to a new appreciation of midcentury modern. Swartz considered replacing the dining room's crystal chandelier with an Art Deco version but realized that the room "would look like a 1930s movie theater," so he chose a 1960s aluminum fixture instead. He has filled out his collection with vintage 1950s pieces, furnishing the breakfast room with a 1956 Tulip table and chairs by Eero Saarinen and the master bedroom with George Nelson's Thin Edge bed.

But Swartz and Johnson are far from being purists. Throughout the house are furnishings collected over the past two decades that span the late 1920s to the 1950s. "It's fun to mix it up," says Johnson. In the living area, a side table by Donald Deskey, a boxy armchair by Paul Frankl, and Nelson's fiberglass Swaged Leg chairs happily coexist—grouped as if to underscore their shared roots in the evolution of modern American design.

beginner's luck

Brandon Webster is typical of many midcentury collectors. Since buying inexpensive 1950s kitsch from thrift stores and estate sales, the young Washington, D.C., photographer has graduated to classic designs. He started his collection in the early 1990s and slowly acquired mass-produced pieces from the typical 1950s home. Among his most prized possessions are pristine wood cabinets from Paul McCobb's Planner Group, purchased from their original owner; a blond corner cabinet made by Heywood-Wakefield; and a glass-topped coffee table on a biomorphic base.

Webster attributes his interest in midcentury design to growing up in the shadow of Cranbrook Academy, near Detroit, where Eero Saarinen, Harry Bertoia, and the Eameses trained. "I always admired its architecture," he says. "This furniture is a progression from Cranbrook. I like the sculptural elements and the clean, strong lines." Since buying his first items for himself, Webster has begun to sell a few of his finds to local dealers.

The 1941 home he purchased in 1996 has spurred his recent collecting. One of ten brick row houses on a block facing Rock Creek Park, the three-story structure was designed by the Washington architects Julian Berla and Joseph Abel, who were responsible for some of the capital's earliest modern apartment blocks.

After living in small spaces, Webster finally has room to spread out his collection on three floors. A Danish wall unit that was in storage for three years now frames the dining room, and a George Nelson Bubble lamp came in exchange for his photographic services. At the center of the space is a vintage Tulip dining set designed by Eero Saarinen for Knoll. Not exactly, Webster explains. The 1956 chairs are authentic, but the table is a knockoff. Only a seasoned collector could tell the difference.

Behind a Nelson Bubble lamp, Webster's Danish hanging cabinet (opposite) displays vintage cameras, glassware, and Scandinavian candlesticks. It is flanked by a 1950s painting and Nelson's Ball clock. Saarinen's pedestal set is the room's centerpiece. Other furnishings in the photographer's row house (left) are a coffee table inspired by Isamu Noguchi (above) placed near the hearth.

161

modernist summit

A sweeping steel staircase (below) leads from the living area, with its Hans Wegner Ox chair, to the rooftop pavilion (opposite). Serge Mouille's spidery 1950s chandelier illuminates the sitting room, where 1940s armchairs by T. H. Robsjohn-Gibbings face a Scandinavian segmented table. On the Paul McCobb table at left is a 1960 lamp with a pivoting reflector by George Nelson.

"I love the idea of good design for the masses," says the New York architect Lee Mindel. "Architects like Charles Eames were providing the middle class with beautiful furniture at a reasonable price." Mindel, however, admits that his favorite midcentury modern furnishings are not manufactured American designs but custom pieces from Europe that are harder to find. Since 1988 he has amassed an unusual collection of architect-designed furnishings from France, Scandinavia, Italy, and Great Britain.

Mindel kept his "compulsive collecting tendencies" under wraps for years. He did not have space for his finds and ended up stashing them in storage crates and basements. His passion finally took over in 1994, when he decided to design an apartment around his possessions atop a former hat factory in Manhattan's Flatiron district. Collaborating with his partner Peter Shelton and the architect Reed Morrison, Mindel renovated the top floor as a combination living quarters and gallery.

Crisply outlined white walls and sliding doors frame spacious rooms that allow him to display and reconfigure the furnishings. Exposed columns, metal-framed glass panels, and a curvy steel staircase leading to a rooftop pavilion recall the loft's industrial past. Within the spare setting, furnishings are pulled away from the walls to show off their sculptural shapes.

In the living room, pieces by the French designers Jean Prouvé and Charlotte Perriand and the Scandinavian designers Hans Wegner, Poul Kjaerholm, and Fritz Henningsen are artfully grouped as if in conversation. "It's like a modernist summit talk," says Mindel, pointing to the black curves of a Serge Mouille chandelier and an Arne Jacobsen chair in the rooftop sitting room. Complementing their simple lines and neutral tones are steel-framed glass tables and rubberized linen carpets designed by Shelton, Mindel.

"Each of these objects embodies the architect's philosophy," reflects Mindel. "Their economy of form inspires my own work." Since completing his loft in 1997, Mindel has shared his expertise to his clients, persuading them to fill their houses and apartments with vintage modern furnishings.

And he has continued to expand his own collection. A recent acquisition is a glass-and-steel table by Oscar Niemeyer, architect of Brazil's capital, Brasilia. But don't expect to see this rare item in current views of Mindel's apartment—the table is still in storage until he finds the perfect place to put it.

A leather-covered bench by Poul Kjaer-holm in the living area (left) stretches next to a Shelton, Mindel glass-and-steel table and an Antonio Citterio sofa. Past Jean Prouvé's circular table is a 1930s wing chair by Fritz Henningsen, a Prouvé console, and a Serge Mouille lamp. Wegner's Ox chairs define the sitting area (above), with its 1950s kite lamp by Pierre Guariche. On the fireplace mantel in front of a 1952 wall unit by Prouvé, Perriand, and Delaunay is a terra-cotta Primavera vase (right).

city deco, country classic

HEINER M. KROMER · SOUTHAMPTON, NEW YORK · 1982

"Early on in my career, I competed with George Nelson," says Joel Portugal, a retired graphic designer who invented identity programs for such corporations as Citibank, Texaco, and American Express. "We were the upstarts. We looked at Nelson as outdated." Now Portugal and his wife, Helen, enjoy cohabiting with Nelson, relaxing on his chairs and benches and using furniture by his postwar American and European colleagues.

The couple began seriously acquiring French Art Deco furniture in the 1980s, decorating their Manhattan apartment with pieces by Jean-Michel Frank, Emile Ruhlman, and other prominent designers. "By 1989 it was complete," notes Helen Portugal. But their collecting was far from over.

Offering enough room for visiting children and grandchildren, a rambling, glass-walled house in Southampton, New York—designed and built by a luggage company magnate in 1982—became their new family getaway. "When I first saw it, I felt as though I had stepped into the house in Alfred Hitchcock's *North by Northwest,*" notes Helen Portugal. She quickly realized that the open spaces, interrupted only by timbers and stone fireplaces inspired by Frank Lloyd Wright, would form the perfect setting for light, organic midcentury furnishings.

While the house was being updated by the New York architect Walter Chatham, the Portugals set about acquiring postwar treasures as intensely as they had collected Deco. Browsing antiques shows and consulting with prominent New York dealers such as Linn Weinberg, they began learning about midcentury designs. "I don't like to buy without knowing the history of a piece," says Helen Portugal.

Framed in wood, the Portugals' rambling glass house (below) reflects a mid-century attitude. In the lower living room (right), the sofa and armchairs are reproductions of 1930s Jean-Michel Frank designs. Light comes from Greta Grossman's tiered lamp and an Otto Kolb lamp, which is atop a 1950s end table by Milo Baughman. George Nakashima's three-legged table sits adjacent to Paul Frankl's cork-topped coffee table. In between the chairs is a Paul Laszlo table.

In the living room (far left) are sofas and chairs by T. H. Robsjohn-Gibbings, a round Florence Knoll table, a Nelson slatted bench, and Greta Grossman's interlocking tables with a planter. The living area (left top) features a Prouvé-Perriand storage unit behind Osvaldo Borsani's 1954 lounge chair. The guest bedroom (left bottom) is furnished with a Frankl desk and a Grossman chair. In the foyer (above) , a Prouvé light fixture extends over 1952 Perriand shelving and a chair by Robsjohn-Gibbings.

Installed throughout the house is a sophisticated mix of mass-produced and one-of-a-kind pieces from America, France, and Scandinavia. Armchairs are by T. H. Robsjohn-Gibbings and—yes—George Nelson; lighting includes rare fixtures by Jean Prouvé and Poul Henningsen, and scattered on top of period tables and cabinets is pottery by Gunnar Nylund and Carl-Harry Stalhane. Instead of framing the furniture against a neutral backdrop of white, the Portugals painted each room a different shade: lime green in the living room, bright blue in the hallway, lavender and melon in the bedrooms. "We based it on the rich colors in the work of Gio Ponti and Le Corbusier," explains Chatham.

One of the collection's unique aspects is that many of the designs are by women: shelving by Charlotte Perriand, lamps and chairs by Greta Grossman, tables by Florence Knoll, and dishes by Eva Zeisel. In the dining room is a walnut table made by Mira Nakashima after a design by her famous father, George Nakashima, whose sideboard is behind it.

The contrast between Art Deco's precious woods and midcentury's plywood and fiberglass does not seem to matter to the Portugals. "There's an elegance to both periods," Helen Portugal maintains. "It fascinates me that the mass-produced designs of the 1950s didn't preclude a high aesthetic level—real beauty."

A Serge Mouille chandelier hangs over the dining table, made by Mira Nakashima after a design by her father, George, who created the sideboard. It features ceramics by Gunnar Nylund and Carl-Harry Stalhane. Hans Wegner designed the chairs—known as The Chair—in 1949. The table is set with Eva Zeisel's 1946–47 Town and Country plates as well as Georg Jensen flatware.

nordic harmony

PHILIP TRUCHAUD · WASHINGTON, D.C. · 1955

Arranged on a flokoti rug in the sitting area (opposite) are a T. H. Robsjohn-Gibbings daybed and his curvy glass coffee table plus a Paddleback chair by Hans Wegner. Lighting includes a 1962 metal Arco lamp and 1950s floor lamps. The far rug is a 1960s design by Wolf Breuer. Carl Aubock did the 1950s tripod table, and Lisa Larson created the ceramic lion sculpture for Gustavsberg.

Artistic integrity means everything to the painter Robin Rose and his wife, Judy Penski, a dentist in Washington, D.C. Since the 1980s the couple has collected midcentury modern furnishings with an eye to originality. In their living room is a daybed designed by T. H. Robsjohn-Gibbings, complete with its tweedy 1954 fabric. Nearby is an Akari lamp by Isamu Noguchi, its rounded paper shade torn in a few places. Planted in the dining area are Eero Saarinen's pedestal table and chairs with bits of foam rubber padding peaking out from the upholstery.

Rose and Penski compare such signs of age to the patina on a fine work of art. Replacing any of the furnishings' worn but historic elements would mean losing authenticity. Buying reproductions is out of the question. "I'm an artist," Rose says. "I don't like people copying my work, so why would I buy a copy of someone else's design?"

A former rock musician, Rose likens each purchase to a note that must harmonize with the rest of the collection. "It has to sing," he says. Scandinavian and Japanese wood furnishings set a handcrafted tone attuned to the house's leafy setting on a hill overlooking Rock Creek Park.

In the living area, a sideboard by George Nakashima strikes a chord with chairs by the Danish designer Hans Wegner and the husband-and-wife team of Nanna and Jorgen Ditzel. Curvaceous molded-plywood benches by Sori Yanagi echo the sculptural chair by the Danish designers Orla Molgaard Nielsen and Peter Hvidt and a table by Finn Juhl. Varying the theme of these warm finishes are abstract paintings by Rose and Jonathan Lasker of New York, rya rugs from Scandinavia, and glass vases by the Japanese artist Toshichi Iwata in various shades of green.

Floating along the room's far wall above a 1954 cabinet designed by the noted woodworker George Nakashima, Rose's earthy encaustic paintings (left) complement a 1950s Veach ceramic vessel.

Perpendicular to the fireplace (left), a Paul McCobb shelving unit holds bronze vessels by Carl Aubock and Sori Yanagi's 1956 butterfly stools. A paper-shaded Akari lamp by Noguchi lights the space. The child's birch plywood rocking horse is from Creative Playthings. Supported on a Viking-inspired base, a teak grandmother's clock (above) in the foyer is a 1960s Danish design by Hovmand-Olsen.

175

The family's glass collection includes colorful vases from the 1950s and 1960s by the Japanese artist Toshichi Iwata (above) and the 1966 Bolle series by Tapio Wirkkala of Finland for Venini (left). In a nearby nook (opposite), Poul Kjaerholm's 1965 caned Hammock chair and Hans Wegner's 1950 Wishbone chair perch in front of the windows. The lamp is by Serge Mouille, and the glass-topped trestle table is Danish. Above the Saarinen pedestal table is a painting by the writer William Burroughs. Beyond Swedish rya rugs from the 1960s, accordion doors to the library allow a peak at a Nelson Bubble lamp.

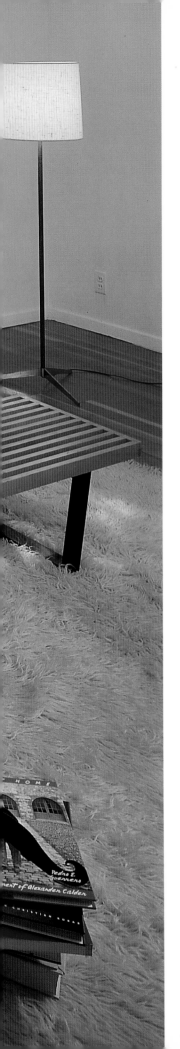

Although Rose and Penski are loath to alter their vintage furnishings, they had no qualms about renovating portions of the 1955 house, which they bought in 1995. Consulting the architect's original plans, they restored the front terraces and installed a glass door from the kitchen to a side patio. After redoing the kitchen down to new cork floors, they repaired the back deck and finished it in slate with glass panels that serve as skylights to Rose's painting studio below.

Within the airy rooms, the furniture is often rearranged and selectively expanded with new purchases. Rose has become a dealer in midcentury modern furnishings, selling his wares from a cooperative store in downtown Washington. Many of his estate-sale bargains are stashed in his basement awaiting transfer to the shop, but some find a permanent home in the upper reaches of the house. These days, Rose is particularly taken with the "comfort and quietude" of Danish modern design—a repose he calls Zen Modern. No matter if the furniture has a scratch. As he notes, "It's the essence of the original design that is important."

The Rose-Penski guest bedroom (left) in Washington is furnished with Hans Wegner's 1950 rope-slung lounge chair, a sewing table, and a daybed. The slatted bench is George Nelson's 1946 classic. A Finnish cooperative wove the rya rug in the 1950s. Silver barware (right) was designed by Arne Jacobsen for Georg Jensen, while the glasses and bottle are from the Swedish firm Holmgaard.

Next to the kitchen pass-through, Eero Saarinen's 1956 Tulip dining table and chairs occupy the center of the dining room (opposite). The small table is also part of Saarinen's fiberglass series. Two of Rose's paintings hang over a 1950s Danish sideboard. The large glass bottle is from Orrefors of Sweden. Arne Jacobsen created the stainless-steel coffee pot and tea service (below) as part of his 1967 Cylinda line for Stelton. The stainless-steel flatware (right) is by Magnus Stevenson for Georg Jensen.

midcentury maverick

"Some of the best design in the world was being done by Americans after the war," says Mark McDonald. "Architects were working with new technology to create furniture that people could afford." A midcentury modern pioneer who is a collector, dealer, and scholar, McDonald has immersed himself in the postwar period for two decades. The current popularity of architect-designed furniture from the 1940s and 1950s—by the likes of Charles and Ray Eames, Isamu Noguchi, Eero Saarinen, and others—can be traced in good part to him.

McDonald first gained his design instincts while working for the New York antiques doyenne Lillian Nassau in the late 1970s. "She taught me the importance of research and documentation," he notes. While he originally wanted to focus his own collecting on Art Deco, McDonald quickly realized that he could not afford first-rate pieces. He then found the undiscovered (and affordable) territory of midcentury modern furniture.

"I had the means to buy the best," recalls McDonald, who soon turned his growing expertise into a business. In 1983 he established the New York store Fifty/50 with partners Ralph Cutler and Mark Isaacson. The shop flourished as artists and design-savvy shoppers recognized the beauty and value of vintage modern pieces. Adding to the cachet were special exhibitions of furniture and art jewelry, complete with catalogues. But Fifty/50 closed in 1993 after the AIDS epidemic felled Cutler and Isaacson.

From his bed, covered in a midcentury Dutch blanket, McDonald can view the Con Edison Tower (left). Over an Eames plywood lounge chair (opposite) are 1941 watercolors by the Pennsylvania painter Lloyd Ney. Norman Bel Geddes designed the black-enamel, aluminum-trimmed chest in the 1930s. The 1950s floor lamp is by Mathieu Buffet, and the 1949 wood and metal stool is by Isamu Noguchi to accompany his Rudder dining table.

Eames storage units divide the living area (opposite) from the dining area's Noguchi Rudder table and stool. The large 1950s ceramic vessel is by Leza McVey, while the 1950 glass vase is by Vicke Lindstrand as part of his Manhattan series for Kosta. In McDonald's Gansevoort Gallery in New York, he sells pots such as Stig Lindberg's stoneware (above) and Axel Salto's organic stoneware bottle (left) and vase (right).

For two years, McDonald dealt privately before opening his Gansevoort Gallery in 1995. Now focused on glass and ceramics, the Texas-born dealer regularly showcases sculptural pieces by Scandinavian artists of the 1950s. He is particularly taken with organic stoneware made by the Danish potter Axel Salto and the American Leza McVey. Several of their vessels are on display in McDonald's Manhattan loft, along with the classic modern furnishings that he lives with. He dines on a three-legged Noguchi table, relaxes on Gio Ponti's aluminum chairs, and sleeps on a bed designed by Norman Bel Geddes for Simmons. On weekends, McDonald retreats to a 1960 split-level in upstate New York. Nicknamed "Runningwater" after Frank Lloyd Wright's celebrated Fallingwater, the house is sited next to a creek and filled with Wrightian and Arts and Crafts furniture.

"Lately, I've been bringing in things that are more comfortable," he explains, pointing to oak-and-leather Spanish chairs designed in Denmark by Borge Mogensen in 1959 and a sofa by Edward Wormley from the same era. McDonald's favorite pieces? He especially likes Noguchi's Rudder table and Ray and Charles Eames's metal Storage Units. "It has nothing to do with their value," he asserts, noting that an original Eames unit in pristine condition now fetches $35,000. "I love their mix of metal, wood, and colors. The spareness of their design appeals to me."

Marcel Breuer's bent-plywood Isokon tables from 1936 (above) nest on a hooked rug inspired by 1930s linoleum. On top are a glass bowl by Fulvio Bianco for Venini and the Swedish designer Stig Lindberg's ceramic Domino dish, both from the 1950s. An Eames plywood screen and a Noguchi Akari lamp (right) frame the living area and a 1948 Nelson sofa. Virginia Berresford's 1934 painting hangs over a Frank Lloyd Wright Usonian table. In the corner is a 1939 version of Kem Weber's 1934 Airline armchair made for Disney Studios.

186

modern necessities

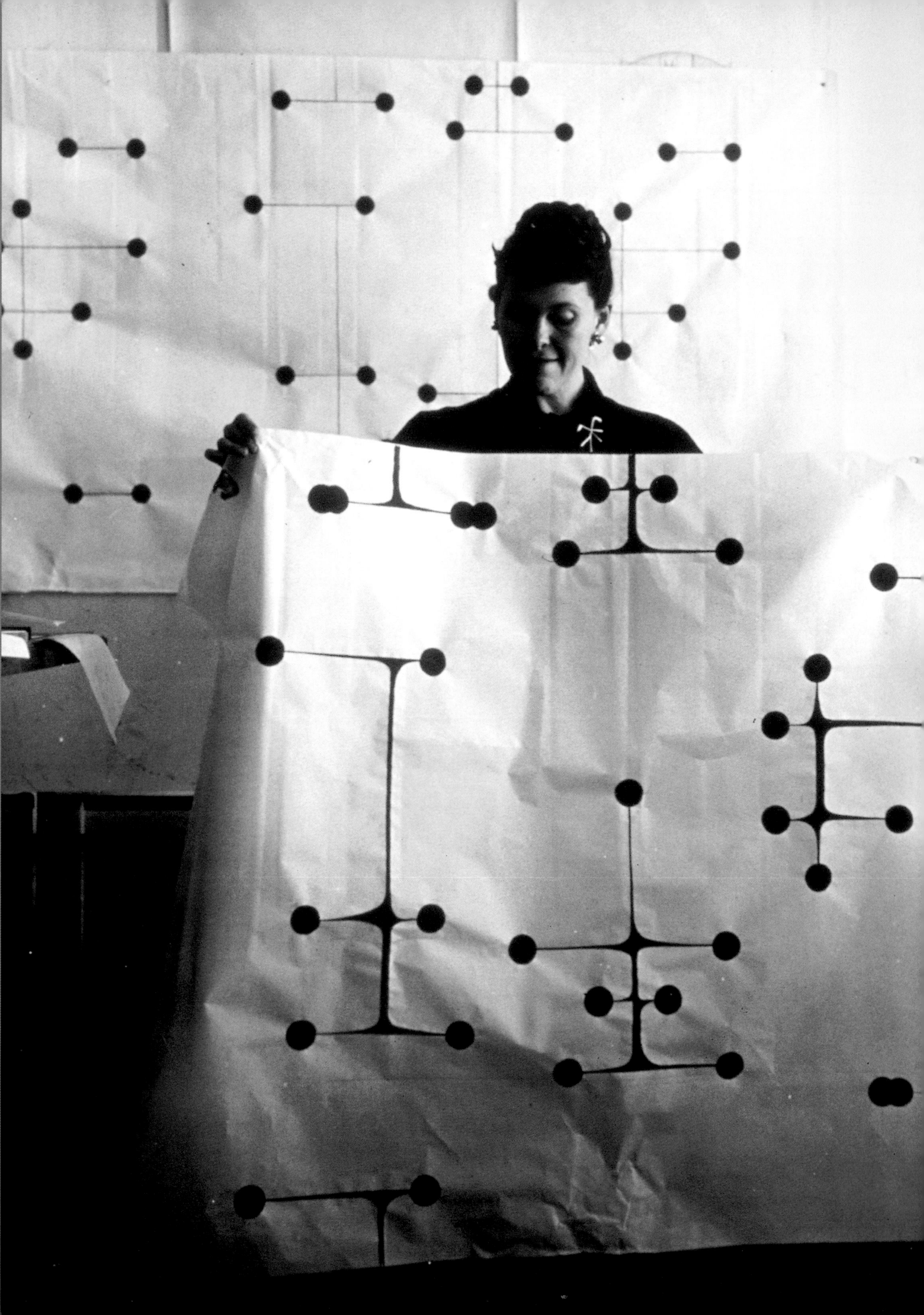

Henningsen Snowball Lamp

a. This classic cascading lamp projects abundant light, while its stepped shades conceal the bulb from every angle. Poul Henningsen, 1924. Louis Poulsen Lighting.

Nelson Marshmallow Sofa

b. The 18 individual "marshmallows" can be detached for easy cleaning and rotated for even wear. George Nelson, 1956. Upolstered cushions in fabric or leather on a tubular steel frame. Herman Miller.

Eames Walnut Stools

c. The three versions of this stool were designed as low tables for the Time-Life Building in New York City and used also throughout the Eameses' home. Ray Eames, 1960. Solid walnut. Herman Miller.

Eames Armchair Shell Rocker

d. The couple's popular molded-fiberglass chair was issued early on in a version with rockers. Charles and Ray Eames, 1950. Fiberglass, chrome, and wood. Modernica.

Mathsson Pernilla 3 Chair

e. This sinuous chaise comes with plaited hemp bands or upholstered in sheepskin over webbing. Bruno Mathsson, 1944. Laminated beech. Scandinavian Design.

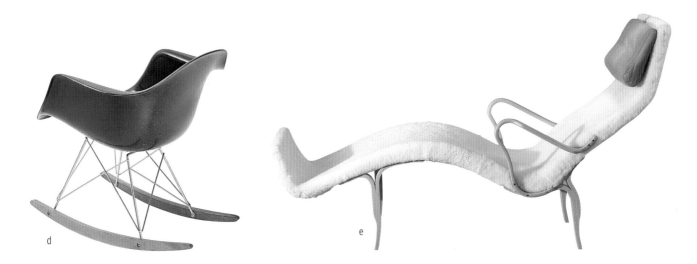

a

b

c

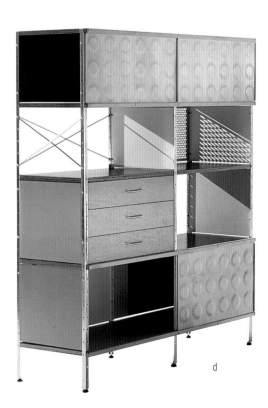

d

Nelson Sunburst Clock

a. George Nelson's bold timepieces resembling heavenly bodies became the clocks of choice at midcentury. George Nelson, 1948–52. Also available: Ball, Asterisk, and Star designs. Vitra Design Museum.

Wegner Ox Chair

b. With its distinctive headrest, this chair drew on ideas first expressed in the designer's Cow Horn and Bull Horn chairs. Hans Wegner, 1960. Leather or Danish fabrics. Design Selections International.

Jacobsen Seven Chairs

c. Now widely imitated, this stacking chair comes in variations with writing arms and casters. Arne Jacobsen, 1955. Laminated wood with metal legs. Fritz Hansen.

Eames Storage Units

d. These lively modular units were an early solution to the problem of creative storage. Charles and Ray Eames, 1950. Various sizes and colors. Molded plywood and zinc-coated steel. Herman Miller.

Heywood-Wakefield Skyliner Night Stand

e. Part of the company's historic Streamline series of furnishings, this bedside stand can be paired with similar items. 1930s–50s. Solid birch. Heywood-Wakefield.

e

191

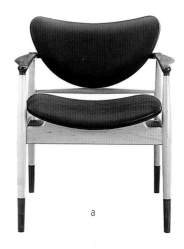

a

b

c

Juhl Sculpted Armchair

a. A soft leather seat and back are suspended between between simple walnut arms that taper into maple legs and walnut feet. Finn Juhl, 1951. Baker Furniture.

Eames Lounge Chair and Ottoman

b. Perhaps the most celebrated pieces of midcentury furniture, this popular pair was crafted for the film director Billy Wilder. Charles and Ray Eames, 1956. Cherry shell with black leather. Herman Miller.

Aalto Stacking Stools

c. Anticipating the stacking plywood furniture of the 1950s, these classic stools, usable also as simple side tables, were designed for the Viipuri Library. Alvar Aalto, 1930. Laminated birch. Artek/Full Upright Position/MoMA Design Store.

Risom Lounge Chair

d. Parachute webbing that failed World War II strength standards did not go to waste: paired with restrained Nordic design, it was used for inventive chair straps. Jens Risom, 1941. Maple and cotton. Knoll.

Bertoia Barstool

e. Part of a series of steel-wire furniture, these tall stools "mainly made of air, like sculpture" are suitable for use indoors as well as outdoors. Harry Bertoia, 1952. Various finishes and cushion colors. Knoll.

d

e

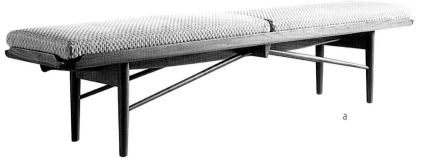

Juhl Cocktail Table–Bench

a. Angled stretchers between tapered legs distinguish this multipurpose table, which converts to a bench. Finn Juhl, 1951. Walnut with a sycamore top. Baker Furniture.

Girard Pillows

b. Designed by the former textile design director of Herman Miller, these pillows feature geometric and folk-art patterns. Alexander Girard, 1957–64. Silkscreened European linen cases stuffed with duck feathers and down. Herman Miller.

Juhl Cocktail Table

c. Atop a tripod base, this unusual tabletop is enhanced with a sycamore veneer field bordered by a contrasting walnut gallery. Finn Juhl, 1951. Baker Furniture.

Robsjohn-Gibbings Strap Stool

d. Wartime cotton webbing proved popular for furniture items, including this small footstool. T. H. Robsjohn-Gibbings, 1954. Wood with metal legs. John Widdicomb.

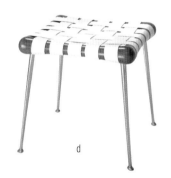

Zeisel Town and Country Dinnerware

e. The Hungarian-born designer's voluptuous Town and Country line of ceramics was originally created for Red Wing Pottery. Eva Zeisel, 1950s. Various pieces and colors. Metropolitan Museum of Art.

a

b

c

d

e

Bertoia Diamond Chair

a. This screenlike chair in which "space passes through," formed of tough steel wire, is available with a padded seat or unupholstered. Harry Bertoia, 1952. Knoll.

Jacobsen Egg Chair

b. Featuring a back, seat, and arms constructed of a single piece of molded foam upholstery, this sculptural chair was created for the SAS Royal Hotel in Copenhagen. Arne Jacobsen, 1958. Fritz Hansen.

Nelson Asterisk Clock

c. Similar to the designer's Star clock, this chunky kitchen favorite is one of four now brought back as reproductions. George Nelson, 1948–52. Vitra Design Museum.

Eames Folding Wooden Screen

d. World War II wood-molding technology was used to create this room divider whose wood sections are joined by mesh bands. Charles and Ray Eames, 1946. Various woods and finishes. Herman Miller.

Robsjohn-Gibbings Iron Board Desk

e. Classical and modern forms are combined to produce a sleek machine for writing. T. H. Robsjohn-Gibbings, 1943–56. Natural or bleached walnut. John Widdicomb.

Saarinen Tulip Tables and Chairs

a. Sculptural pedestals solved the problem of having a "slum of legs" underfoot. Eero Saarinen, 1956. Various sizes and cushion colors. White plastic laminate; oval or round tabletops, marble optional. Knoll.

Eames Sofa Compact

b. This foldable sofa evolved from one designed for the couple's California home. Charles and Ray Eames, 1954. Foam cushions on chrome-plated legs. Herman Miller.

Noguchi Table

c. Designed by a sculptor, this biomorphic table balances form and practical function. Isamu Noguchi, 1948. Plate glass with walnut or ebonized base. Herman Miller.

Eames Molded-Plywood Lounge Chair

d. This chair, formed using revolutionary wood-molding techniques, was made to fit the body's contours. Charles and Ray Eames, 1946. Plywood. Red, ebony, and other finishes and veneers. Herman Miller.

Noguchi Akari Light Sculpture

e. Based on traditional Japanese lanterns, this is one of many Akari ("light") lamps developed from the sculptor's original three-legged 1948 design. Isamu Noguchi, 1951. Various shapes and sizes. Paper, bamboo, and metal. Noguchi Foundation.

195

Heywood-Wakefield StyleMaster Bed

a. Part of a large bedroom ensemble, this bed features a distinctive open footboard. 1930s–50s. Queen, King, and California King sizes. Solid birch. Heywood-Wakefield.

Wegner Wishbone Chair

b. Inspired by Asian furniture, this armchair, variously called the Y chair, followed a Chinese design of 1943. Hans Wegner, 1950. Design Selections International.

Saarinen Womb Chair

c. This classic and comforting chair, one of the most popular midcentury pieces still in production, fits its name. Eero Saarinen, 1948. Various upholstery colors with a pillow and metal base. Knoll.

Robsjohn-Gibbings Lounge Chair

d. Ancient Greek design inspired the look of this elegant chair. T. H. Robsjohn-Gibbings, 1946. Solid walnut frame with upholstered cushions. John Widdicomb.

Jacobsen Ant Chair

e. Designed for the Novo Pharmaceutical Company dining room in Denmark, this stackable single-shell chair takes its name from its insectlike demeanor. Arne Jacobsen, 1952. Various finishes. Fritz Hansen.

a

Nelson Bubble Lamp

a. This saucer-shaped hanging lamp is part of a series inspired by mothballed ships. George Nelson, 1952. Translucent plastic over a wire frame. Herman Miller.

Cracked-Ice Dinette Set

b. Classic midcentury kitchen furniture is available again in a wide array of styles and materials. Each set is custom made. 1954. Laminate and chrome. Pastense.

Eames Molded-Plywood Coffee Table

c. Nicknamed "the dish," this indented-top table with curved wooden legs complements the Eameses' molded-plywood chairs. Charles and Ray Eames, 1946. Veneered plywood. Herman Miller.

Vinyl Bar Stool

d. A variety of bar stools, all custom made, recapture the colorful yet practical favorites that furnished 1950s luncheonettes. Laminate and chrome. Pastense.

Eames Elliptical Table

e. Sometimes called the Surfboard table, this aerodynamic coffee table is a larger version of the couple's 1950 wire-base table. Charles and Ray Eames, 1951. Laminated birch with a wire base. Herman Miller.

b

c

d

e

Jacobsen Swan Chair

a. Like the designer's Egg chair, this equally organic chair was created for the SAS Royal Hotel lobby. Arne Jacobsen, 1958. Molded polyurethane. Fritz Hansen.

Heywood-Wakefield Madeline Club Chair

b. One of several armchairs and davenports put back into production by the company, this piece typifies the overstuffed look. 1930s–50s. Various solid and geometric fabrics. Heywood-Wakefield.

Bertoia Bird Chair and Ottoman

c. This upholstered chair set is part of the designer's steel-wire series, created the same year as his more famous Diamond chair. Harry Bertoia, 1952. Knoll.

Nelson Platform Bench

d. Casting shadows like a screen, this slatted platform was designed as the base for Nelson's Basic Cabinet series but has long been used as a bench. George Nelson, 1946. Maple or ebony finish. Herman Miller.

Eames Molded-Plywood Dining Chair

e. A variation on the Eameses' plywood designs, this dining chair with metal legs was developed from three-legged prototypes. Charles and Ray Eames, 1946. Various veneers and finishes. Herman Miller.

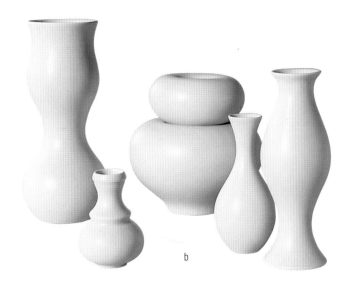

Noguchi Dinette Table

a. In this table designed by the noted sculptor, a fan of slender chrome legs supports a round tabletop. Isamu Noguchi, 1954. Laminate or maple top. Modernica.

Zeisel Vases

b. Zeisel describes her work as "the playful search for beauty." These new vases continue her organic forms begun a half century ago. Eva Zeisel, 1990s. KleinReid.

Eames Hang-It-All

c. The Eameses delighted in making children's furniture and toys. This colorful hanging rack reveals their whimsical side. Charles and Ray Eames, 1953. Steel rods with solid maple knobs. Herman Miller.

Yanagi Butterfly Stool

d. Japanese design meets Western manufacturing techniques in this delicate stool whose sides reach upward like arms. Sori Yanagi, 1956. Molded plywood and steel. Tendo Mokko/MoMA Design Store.

Miniature Chairs

e. Each of these miniatures—by Aalto, Bertoia, and the Eameses—is handcrafted using the same materials as the originals but at one-sixth of their full size. Various materials. Vitra Design Museum.

resources

Scandinavian Design

347 Fifth Avenue, Suite 1009

New York, N.Y. 10016

p: 212-213-0009/f: 212-684-7931

w: scandinaviandesigninc.com

Vitra Design Museum

204 Pennsylvania Avenue, Suite B

Easton, Md. 21601

p: 410-763-7698/f: 410-820-7771

w: www.vitra.com

Vladimir Kagan Design Group

1185 Park Avenue

New York, N.Y. 10128

p: 212-289-0031/f: 212-360-7307

w: www.vladimirkagan.com

FEATURED ARCHITECTS

Barry Berkus

Berkus Design Studio

2020 Alameda Padre Serra, Suite 133

Santa Barbara, Calif. 93103

p: 805-963-8901

Case Study House No. 9

Walter Chatham and Evans Simpson

Walter Chatham Architect

580 Broadway

New York, N.Y. 10012

p: 212-925-2202

Portugal House

John Howey

John Howey and Associates

121 West Whiting Street

Tampa, Fla. 33602

p: 813-223-5396

Umbrella House

Huson Jackson

Sert Jackson and Associates

442 Marrett Road, Suite 10

Lexington, Mass. 02421

p: 781-863-5711

Sert House

Dirk Lohan

Lohan Associates

225 North Michigan Avenue

Chicago, Ill. 60601

p: 312-938-4455

Farnsworth House

Leo Marmol and Ron Radziner

Marmol and Radziner Architecture + Construction

2902 Nebraska Avenue

Santa Monica, Calif. 90404

p: 310-264-1814

Loewy and Kaufmann Houses

Lee Mindel

Shelton, Mindel and Associates

216 West 18th Street

New York, N.Y. 10011

p: 212-243-3939

Mindel Loft

Dion Neutra

Richard and Dion Neutra Architects

2440 Neutra Place

Los Angeles, Calif. 90039

p: 323-666-1806

Camiel House

Kevin Roche

Roche Dinkeloo and Associates

20 Davis Street

Hamden, Conn. 06517

p: 203-777-7251

Miller House

PHOTOGRAPHERS

Kim Ahm: 21, 28–29 both, 45

Allyn Ashmore: 30, 122–27 all

Jonn Coolidge: 165 bottom

Eames Office: 16 bottom, 20 bottom, 188

Michael Freeman: 92–95 all

Dana Gallagher: 68, 69, 70 bottom, 73

David Glomb: front jacket, 7, 9, 26–27 both, 43, 46–51 all, 52–57 all, 96–99 all

John Hall: 182–84 all, 186–87 both

Fritz Hansen: 2–3, 20 top, 33, 208

David Hewitt/Anne Garrison: 133, 142–47 all

Eva Heyd, Gansevoort Gallery: 38, 41 both, 185 all

Matthew Hranek: 80–85 all, 106–7 both

Balthazar Korab: 4–5, 70 top, 71, 72 all

Christian Korab: back jacket, 14, 23, 25, 34, 35, 37, 39, 40, 74–79 all, 87, 108–15 all, 116–21 all, 154–59 all, 166–71 all, 172–81 all

Maharam: case binding, front and back endpapers, 188, 189

Sheila Metzner: 36, 62 left, 65 top

Herman Miller: 100 right

Michael Moran: 162, 163, 164, 165 top

Paul Rocheleau: 58–61 all

Julius Shulman: 6, 8, 10, 16 top, 42

Tim Street-Porter: 1, 13, 17, 32, 63, 64, 65 bottom, 66–67 both, 100 left, 101–5 all, 134–41 all, 148–53 all

Dominique Vorillon: 11, 15, 19, 88–91 all

Marvin Wax: 18, 22

Brandon Webster: 160–61 all

Wilsonart International: 31, 128–31 all

midcentury designers

Harry Bertoia (1915–78). A sculptor, the Italian-born Bertoia studied design at Cranbrook Academy and then joined the faculty to teach metal crafts and graphics. In 1949 he moved to California to work for Charles and Ray Eames. Three years later Bertoia began producing his own metal furniture for Knoll, including his famous Diamond chair. Bertoia described his wire-cage designs as "functional sculpture."

Marcel Breuer (1902–81). Breuer, a student and teacher at the Bauhaus in Germany, is responsible for such 1920s classic furnishings as the tubular Wassily and cantilever-seat Cesca chairs. In 1933 the Hungarian architect moved to England, where he developed bent-plywood furniture. He was invited by Walter Gropius to teach at Harvard University in 1937, and the two formed an architectural practice. In 1949 he designed a model home in the garden of the Museum of Modern Art in New York City. His planar, modern houses grew to incorporate natural materials such as stone and wood. In the 1960s Breuer concentrated on large-scale projects such as the Whitney Museum of American Art in New York.

Charles Eames (1907–78). Eames began his career as an architect in his native St. Louis and became one of the most versatile designers of the twentieth century. He met both his future wife, Ray Kaiser, and Eero Saarinen while teaching at Cranbrook Academy. Eames and Saarinen collaborated on molded-plywood furniture, winning a design competition sponsored by the Museum of Modern Art in 1940. After marrying Ray in 1941, Eames moved to California and began designing plywood splints for the navy. The couple then created revolutionary furniture from plywood, fiberglass, and steel wire and in 1949 built a house from standard industrial building components. In the 1950s the Eameses produced films and traveling exhibits and continued to design furniture. One of the most successful pieces from this period is the 1956 leather-and-rosewood lounge chair and ottoman.

Ray Kaiser Eames (1912–88). Ray Kaiser first studied to be a painter with Hans Hofmann and became a founding member of the American Abstract Artists group. In 1940–41 she attended Cranbrook Academy, where she met Charles Eames. The couple later collaborated on plywood splints and furniture, and Ray applied this technique to create curvilinear sculpture. She developed the settings for the Eameses' furniture and films, as well as fabric designs and the playful style of "orderly clutter" that typified their interiors and graphics. In 1960 Herman Miller produced her line of turned wooden stools.

Craig Ellwood (1922–92). The youngest of the Case Study House architects, Ellwood worked for a building contractor after World War II, where he was exposed to the modern architecture of Wright, Neutra, Saarinen, and Eames. From 1950 to 1954 he studied engineering at the University of California, Los Angeles, while managing his own firm. His three Case Study Houses, developed between 1952 and 1958, typify the structural rigor of his steel-framed architecture. After designing several large-scale projects, Ellwood closed his office in 1977 to paint full time.

Albert Frey (1903–98). The Swiss-born Frey was the first disciple of Le Corbusier to build in the United States. In 1930 he formed a New York–based partnership with A. Lawrence Kocher and produced technically innovative housing in canvas and aluminum. Most of Frey's career was spent in Palm Springs, California, where he developed a modernist style attuned to the desert. One of his most notable contributions is the 1946 courtyard house for Raymond Loewy.

Alexander Girard (1907–93). Inspired by folk art and native cultures, Girard designed joyously patterned fabrics for the progressive furniture created by his colleagues Ray and Charles Eames, George Nelson, and Eero Saarinen. Educated in Europe as an architect, Girard relocated to Detroit in 1937 to work for such clients as the Ford Motor Company on car interiors and product design. In 1952 he became director of design for Herman Miller's textile division, developing new weaves, bright prints, and geometric patterns. He also designed the Museum of Modern Art's *Good Design* exhibitions and colorful designs for Braniff airplanes. His vast folk art collection was donated to the Museum of International Folk Art in Santa Fe.

Charles Goodman (1906–92). Responsible for introducing Washington, D.C., to modern architecture, Goodman designed several innovative suburban communities in the 1950s. His most significant is Hollin Hills in Alexandria, Virginia, undertaken with the developer Robert Davenport. Sited to respect the landscape, Goodman's housing was both experimental and regional. The architect began his career in the 1930s as a government architect, designing the terminal at National Airport (1941) and several federal buildings.

Arne Jacobsen (1901–71). A prolific Danish architect and designer, Jacobsen created furniture, china, glass, flatware, textiles, and lamps. Many of his mass-produced furnishings were originally developed for his buildings. Among his best-known pieces are the sculptural Egg and Swan chairs produced in 1958 for the SAS Royal Hotel in Copenhagen. Of all Scandinavian furnishings, Jacobsen's elegantly curved designs come closest to the organic sensibility of American postwar modernists such as Eames and Saarinen.

Pierre Koenig (b. 1925). Simple and economical, nearly all the buildings designed by Koenig are of steel. The Los Angeles architect started his love affair with the metal when he designed his first house while a student at the University of Southern California. Best known for his famous Case Study Houses nos. 21 and 22, designed in the late 1950s, Koenig has continued to refine prefabricated steel components into powerfully minimalist statements.

Paul McCobb (1917–69). McCobb popularized flexible furniture, room dividers, and storage walls. His low wooden pieces with clean lines were represented at the Museum of Modern Art's *Good Design* exhibitions and sold at department stores. He started his own firm in 1945 to design furniture and fabrics. His most well known line of low-cost furnishings is the modular Planner Group, launched in 1949.

Ludwig Mies van der Rohe (1886–1969). Considered one of the masters of modernism, the German architect Mies van der Rohe designed many influential houses and apartments in Europe in the 1920s and 1930s. Among his most famous works is the German Pavilion at the 1929 International Exhibition in Barcelona, Spain, complete with custom-designed furniture that is still in production. From 1930 to 1933 Mies was a teacher and head of the German Bauhaus until its closure by the Nazis. He came to America in 1938 to head what is now the Illinois Institute of Technology and to develop its

Chicago campus. Mies's Farnsworth House perfectly represents his "less is more" philosophy.

Serge Mouille (1922–88). Trained as a silversmith, this French designer developed adjustable lighting fixtures that resembled mobiles and stabiles beginning in 1953. In addition to lighting, Mouille designed jewelry, graphics, sculpture, and a car chassis in the 1950s.

George Nakashima (1905–90). Nakashima is renowned for crafted wooden furniture emphasizing the intrinsic nature of wood. A graduate of the Massachusetts Institute of Technology, he opened his own workshop in New Hope, Pennsylvania, in 1946. His graceful, simple forms reveal the shape, grain, and bark of a tree and hint at Japanese and Shaker design. Nakashima created a line of furniture for Knoll in the 1940s, but many of his pieces were handmade or produced in small quantities.

George Nelson (1908–86). Trained in architecture at Yale University, he became an editor of *Architectural Forum,* wrote several books, and designed everything from corporate logos to houses. In 1946 Nelson was appointed the first design director at Herman Miller, launching his iconic slatted Platform bench, Coconut chair, and Marshmallow sofa. In 1947 he established his own firm to create molded–melamine dinnerware and space-saving, modular furnishings for the home and office.

Richard Neutra (1892–1970). The Austrian-born architect was influential in introducing modernism to the United States. After arriving in 1923, he briefly worked for Frank Lloyd Wright and then moved to Los Angeles. Beginning with projects such as the Lovell ("Health") House (1929), Neutra expanded his taut, horizontal architecture into the landscape. Among his masterpieces is the 1946 Kaufmann House.

Isamu Noguchi (1904–88). Born in Los Angeles, Noguchi spent his childhood in Japan until 1918, when he returned to the United States. A distinguished sculptor, he is best known for his paper-shaded Akari ("light") lamps. The lanternlike fixtures are still produced in a wide variety of shapes, from simple spheres to complex twists. Noguchi also designed furniture for Knoll and Herman Miller, such as his coffee table composed of a sculptural wooden base and a glass top.

Charlotte Perriand (1903–99). Perriand became a convert to modernism through her work with the French architect Le Corbusier beginning in 1927. She produced many interiors and furnishings, including the tubular-steel chaise longue previously attributed to Corbu. From 1940 to 1946 Perriand lived in Japan and Indochina, creating modern furnishings based on Asian traditions. Working with Jean Prouvé in the 1950s, she turned to prefabricated modular designs.

PICTURED ABOVE (LEFT TO RIGHT): GEORGE NELSON, EDWARD WORMLEY, EERO SAARINEN, HARRY BERTOIA, CHARLES EAMES, AND JENS RISOM.

Gio Ponti (1891–1979). A prolific architect and designer, Ponti propelled Italy back to prominence in the design world during the 1940s and 1950s with textiles, ceramics, glassware, bathroom fixtures, flatware, and furniture—all distinguished by exaggerated, tapering lines. He edited influential design magazines, wrote books, taught, and erected buildings all over the world. Ponti enjoyed modernizing traditional designs, as reflected in his Superleggera ("extra light") chair for Cassina.

Jean Prouvé (1901–84). The son of an Art Nouveau designer, the French architect Jean Prouvé began his career in 1923 as a metalsmith. He collaborated with leading architects such as Robert Mallet-Stevens and Le Corbusier, and in 1936 he designed one of France's first curtain-wall buildings. In the postwar decades he pioneered prefabricated construction systems for housing and schools and applied the same machined approach to furniture design, producing adjustable chairs, tables, and desks with an industrial flair.

Jens Risom (b. 1916). Born in Copenhagen, Risom immigrated to the United States in 1939. He met Hans Knoll in 1941 and created a group of wood-framed chairs upholstered in parachute webbing. After serving in the army, he established his own furniture company in 1946 to produce comfortable modern designs. In the 1960s he focused his business on the growing commercial interiors market.

T. H. Robsjohn-Gibbings (1909–73). Terrance Harold Robsjohn-Gibbings, born in England, combined modern and classical forms to create a unique style. He launched his career in 1936 by moving from London to New York and opening a showroom. His lithe, debonair furnishings, usually framed in light-colored woods, were often based on Greek motifs. In 1946 the Widdicomb Furniture Company produced a group of his pieces, which influenced other designers. "Gibby" published several books attacking traditional and modern design.

Paul Rudolph (1918–97). Educated at Harvard, Rudolph became an influential proponent of regional modernism. In the 1950s he worked in Sarasota, Florida, designing climate-sensitive houses that took advantage of new technologies. From 1958 to 1965 Rudolph chaired Yale's architecture department and designed the university's Art and Architecture Building (1963). He established a New York office in 1966 and spent his later years concentrating on highrise design in Asia.

Eero Saarinen (1910–61). The son of the noted Finnish architect Eliel Saarinen, Eero Saarinen grew up at Cranbrook Academy, where his father taught. After studying sculpture in Paris and architecture at Yale, he returned to Cranbrook and met Charles Eames. After winning the Museum of Modern Art's 1940 furniture competition, Saarinen developed his Womb and Tulip chairs for Knoll. As an architect, he shared a partnership with his father until the elder Saarinen's death in 1950. His furniture and buildings, including the landmark Dulles Airport and TWA Terminal at Kennedy Airport (both 1962), are marked by a structural expressiveness.

José Luis Sert (1902–82). A follower of Le Corbusier, the Spanish-born Sert enriched modern architecture with vernacular and regional influences. In 1937 he designed Spain's pavilion at the Paris world's fair, for which Picasso painted his famous *Guernica.* Two years later he came to the United States and, after working as a town planner, was appointed dean of Harvard's Graduate School of Design in 1953. Sert established partnerships in Boston and designed a wide range of buildings in the United States and abroad.

Hans Wegner (b. 1914). Trained as a cabinetmaker, this Danish designer applied traditional techniques to create modern furniture. His first important design, the 1947 Peacock chair, was a reworking of the Windsor. After working for Arne Jacobsen, he set up his own office in 1943. In the 1950s and 1960s Wegner experimented with molded-plywood shells, metal frames, and string upholstery, but he is best remembered for simple wooden chairs such as the Wishbone and China chairs.

Edward J. Wormley (1907–95). A designer of what he called "transitional" furniture, Wormley combined modern and traditional forms into pieces that were acceptable to a wide audience. After serving as chief designer and design director for Dunbar Furniture Company in the 1930s, he established his firm in New York City in 1945 and created products for Drexel, RCA, and Lightolier as well as Dunbar. His furniture was included in two *Good Design* exhibitions at the Museum of Modern Art.

Sori Yanagi (b. 1915). Best known for his 1956 molded-plywood Butterfly stool, this Japanese designer in 1952 founded an industrial design institute. He later taught at an arts and crafts university in addition to designing ceramics, tableware, plastic furniture, appliances, and tractors.

Eva Zeisel (b. 1906). Recognized for her elegant ceramic dinnerware, the Hungarian-born Zeisel worked for several manufacturers in Germany and Russia before coming to the United States in 1939 to teach at Pratt Institute. In 1946 the Museum of Modern Art exhibited her line of simple white, European-style china. Zeisel designed expressive tableware for Hall and other American manufacturers, as well as wooden objects and furniture. Her work was the subject of a major retrospective in 1984 at the Montreal Museum of Decorative Arts.

Abercrombie, Stanley. *George Nelson: The Design of Modern Design.* Cambridge: MIT Press, 1995.

Albrecht, Donald, ed. *The Work of Charles and Ray Eames: A Legacy of Invention.* New York: Harry N. Abrams, 1997.

Betsky, Aaron, ed. *Sitting on the Edge: Modernist Design from the Collection of Michael and Gabrielle Boyd.* San Francisco: San Francisco Museum of Modern Art, 1998.

Cygelman, Adele. *Palm Springs Modern: Houses in the California Desert.* New York: Rizzoli International Publications, 1999.

Ditto, Jerry, and Lanning Stern. *Design for Living: Eichler Homes.* San Francisco: Chronicle Books, 1995.

Friedman, Alice T. *Women and the Making of the Modern Huose: A Social and Architectural History.* New York: Harry N. Abrams, 1998.

Glancey, Jonathan. *Modern Masters of the 20th-Century Interior.* New York: Rizzoli International Publications, 1999.

Goldstein, Barbara, ed. With essay by Esther McCoy. *Arts + Architecture: The Entenza Years.* Los Angeles: Hennessey and Ingalls, 1998.

Gössel, Peter, ed. *Julius Shulman: Architecture and Its Photography.* Cologne: Taschen, 1998.

Greenberg, Cara. *Mid-Century Modern: Furniture of the 1950s.* New York: Harmony Books, 1984.

Habegger, Jerryll, and Joseph H. Osman. *Sourcebook of Modern Furniture.* W. W. Norton, 1996.

Halberstam, David. *The Fifties.* New York: Villard Books, 1993.

Hess, Alan. *Googie: Fifties Coffee Shop Architecture.* San Francisco, Chronicle Books, 1986.

Hilderbrand, Gary R. *The Miller Garden: Icon of Modernism.* Washington, D.C.: Spacemaker Press, 1999.

Hine, Thomas. *Populuxe.* New York: Alfred A. Knopf, 1986.

Hines, Thomas S. *Richard Neutra and the Search for Modern Architecture.* Berkeley: University of California Press, 1994

Horn, Richard. *Fifties Style Then and Now.* New York: Beech Tree Books, 1985.

Howey, John. *The Sarasota School of Architecture, 1941–1966.* Cambridge: MIT Press, 1995.

Jackson, Lesley. *Contemporary: Architecture and Interiors of the 1950s.* London: Phaidon Press, 1994.

La Pietra, Ugo, ed. *Gio Ponti.* New York: Rizzoli International Publications, 1996.

Masello, David. *Architecture Without Rules: The Houses of Marcel Breuer and Herbert Beckhard.* New York: W. W. Norton, 1993.

McCoy, Esther. *Case Study Houses: 1945–1962.* Los Angeles: Hennessey and Ingalls, 1977.

——. *Craig Ellwood.* 1968. Reprint, Los Angeles: Hennessey and Ingalls, 1998.

Oda, Noritsugu. *Danish Chairs.* San Francisco: Chronicle Books, 1999.

Pile, John. *The Dictionary of 20th-Century Design.* New York: Facts on File, 1990.

Piña, Leslie A. *Alexander Girard Designs for Herman Miller.* Atglen, Pa.: Schiffer Publishing, 1998.

——. *Circa Fifties Glass from Europe and America.* Atglen, Pa.: Schiffer Publishing, 1997.

——. *Classic Herman Miller.* Atglen, Pa.: Schiffer Publishing, 1998.

——. *Fifties Furniture.* Atglen, Pa.: Schiffer Publishing, 1996.

Rapson, Rip, et al. *Ralph Rapson: Sixty Years of Modern Design.* Afton, Minn.: Afton Historical Society Press, 1999.

Rosa, Joseph. *Albert Frey, Architect.* New York: Princeton Architectural Press, 1999.

Sembach, Klaus-Jurgen. *Contemporary Furniture: An International Review of Modern Furniture, 1950 to the Present.* New York: Architectural Book Publishing Company, 1982.

Smith, Elizabeth, ed. *Blueprints for Modern Living: History and Legacy of the Case Study Houses.* Cambridge: MIT Press, 1989.

Steele, James, and David Jenkins. *Pierre Koenig.* London: Phaidon Press, 1998.

Treib, Marc, and Dorothee Imbert. *Garrett Eckbo: Modern Landscapes for Living.* Berkeley: University of California Press, 1997.

index

Page numbers in italics indicate illustrations.

SIMON & SCHUSTER
Rockefeller Center
1230 Avenue of the Americas
New York, NY 10020

Printed in Italy

10   9   8   7   6   5   4   3   2   1

Library of Congress Cataloging-in-Publication Data

Dietsch, Deborah K.
Classic modern: midcentury modern at home / Deborah K. Dietsch
p.   cm.
"An Archetype Press book."
Includes bibliographical references and index.
ISBN 0-684-86744-3
1. Modern movement (Architecture)—United States.
2. Architecture, Modern—20th century—United States. I. Title.
NA 712.5.M63 D54 2000
728′.37′097309045—dc21   00-037051

Produced by Archetype Press, Inc., Washington, D.C.

Diane Maddex, Project Director
Carol Kim, Editorial Assistant
Robert L. Wiser, Designer

Case binding: Dot Pattern fabric by Ray Eames, 1947, manufactured by Maharam. © 2000 Eames Office. Front endleaves: Circles fabric by Ray Eames, 1947, manufactured by Maharam. © 2000 Eames Office. Page 1: Eye clock by George Nelson, 1950s, Friedman collection. Pages 2–3: Ant chairs by Arne Jacobsen, 1952, manufactured by Fritz Hansen. Pages 4–5: Carpet by Alexander Girard for the Miller House, 1957. Page 6: Julius Shulman photograph of Case Study House no. 22 by Pierre Koenig, 1960. Page 7: Case Study House no. 22 today. Page 8: Julius Shulman photograph of Kaufmann House by Richard Neutra, 1947. Page 9: Kaufmann House today. Page 10: Julius Shulman photograph of Case Study House no. 9 by Charles Eames and Eero Saarinen, 1949. Page 11: Case Study House no. 9 today. Page 42: Julius Shulman photograph of Loewy House by Albert Frey, 1947. Page 43: Loewy House today. Page 188: Ray Eames holding Dot Pattern fabric design, 1947. Page 189: Dot Pattern fabric by Ray Eames, 1947, manufactured by Maharam. © 2000 Eames Office. Page 208: PK20 chair by Poul Kjaerholm, 1967, manufactured by Fritz Hansen. Back endleaves: Crosspatch fabric by Ray Eames, 1947, reproduced by Maharam. © 2000 Eames Office.

Acknowledgments

I am indebted to the midcentury "maniacs" who own these houses for sharing their enthusiasm for the period, especially those people who opened their homes to us. Thanks to my editors at the *Sun-Sentinel*—Ellen Soeteber, John Dolen, and Robin Berkowitz—for their encouragement and support. A special thank you goes to my father, Robert W. Dietsch, for his research, as well as to Robin Rose, Ron Crider, John Howey, Mark McDonald, Brandon Webster, Bibi Lamborn, Travis Smith, Coralie Langston Jones, as well as all the photographers and furnishings suppliers. I extend deepest gratitude to Diane Maddex, my editor at Archetype Press, for her patience and persistence.

This book is dedicated to the memory of my mother, Paulene F. Dietsch, who always knew that our Robsjohn-Gibbings furniture was in style.

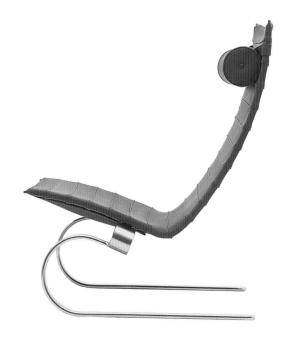

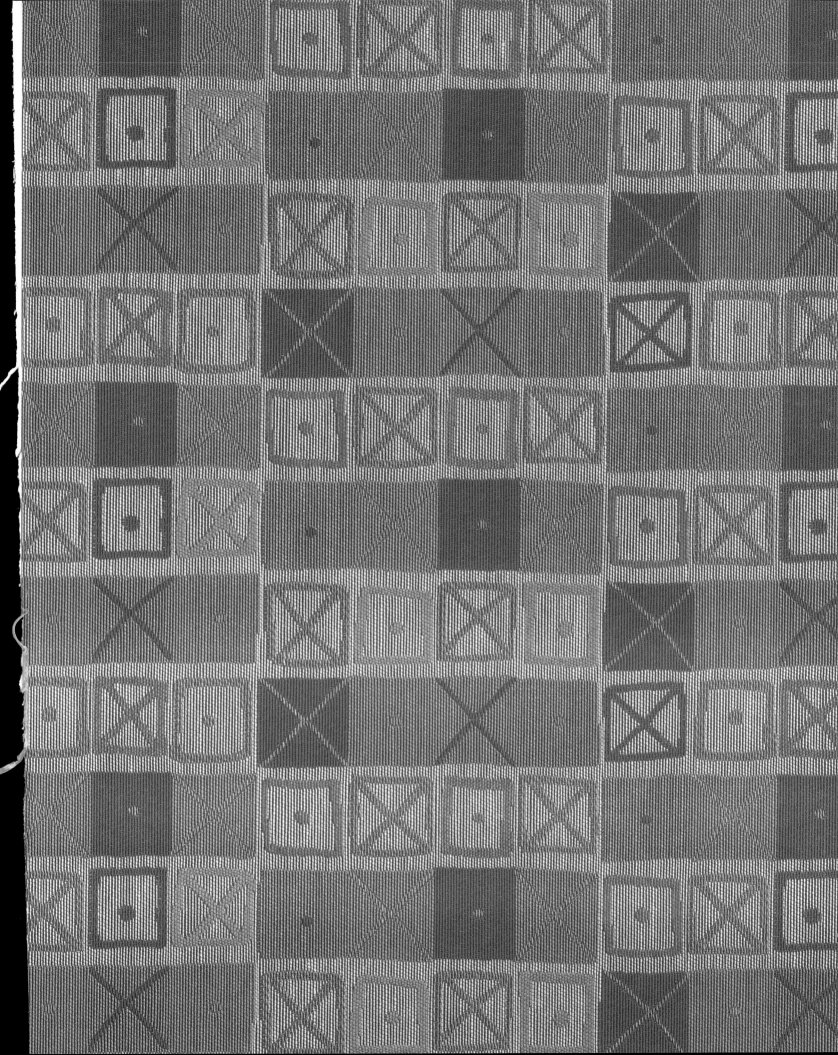

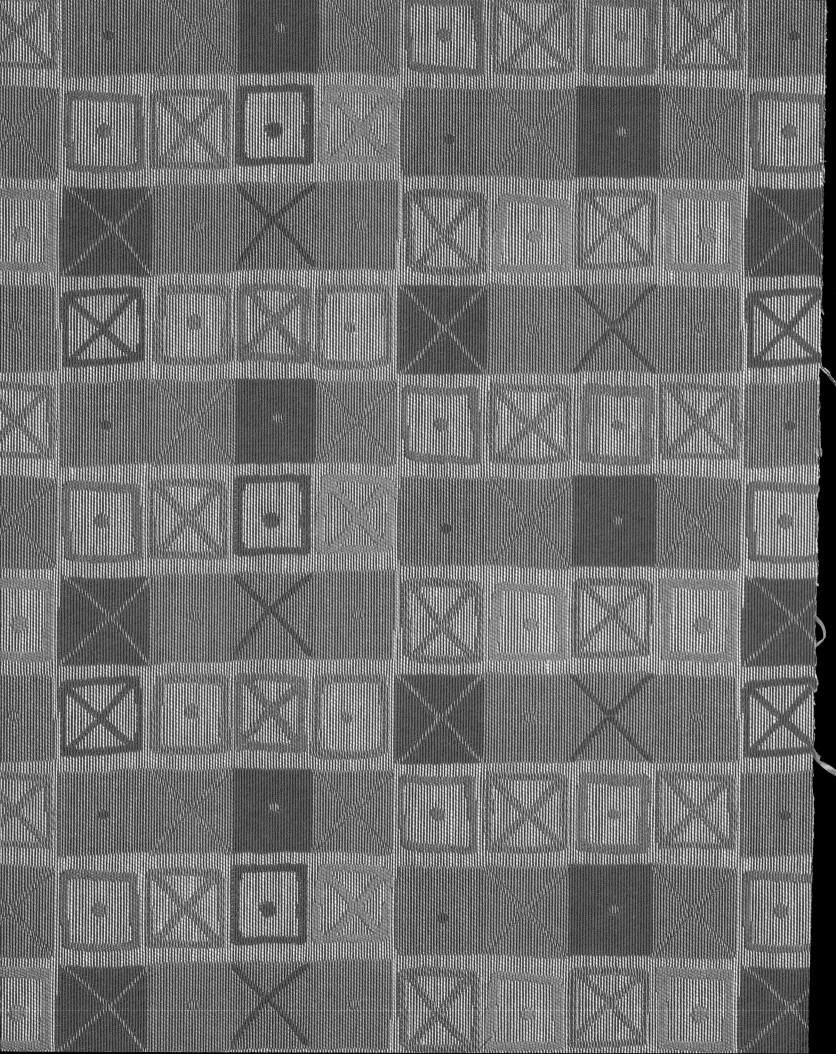